Beyond J

G000078938

Beyond Journalism

Mark Deuze
and Tamara Witschge

polity

Copyright © Mark Deuze and Tamara Witschge 2020

The right of Mark Deuze and Tamara Witschge to be identified as Authors of this Work has been asserted in accordance with the UK Copyright, Designs and Patents Act 1988.

First published in 2020 by Polity Press

Polity Press
65 Bridge Street
Cambridge CB2 1UR, UK

Polity Press
101 Station Landing
Suite 300
Medford, MA 02155, USA

All rights reserved. Except for the quotation of short passages for the purpose of criticism and review, no part of this publication may be reproduced, stored in a retrieval system or transmitted, in any form or by any means, electronic, mechanical, photocopying, recording or otherwise, without the prior permission of the publisher.

ISBN-13: 978-0-7456-4341-0
ISBN-13: 978-0-7456-4342-7(pb)

A catalogue record for this book is available from the British Library.

Library of Congress Cataloging-in-Publication Data
Names: Deuze, Mark, author. | Witschge, Tamara, author.
Title: Beyond journalism / Mark Deuze, Tamara Witschge.
Description: Cambridge, UK ; Medford, MA : Polity, 2019. | Includes
    bibliographical references and index. | Summary: "Among the most significant
    changes affecting journalism is the emergence of startup culture. Through case
    studies of journalism startups, this book provides insight into the promises
    and pitfalls of media entrepreneurship, ultimately recognizing new voices as
    legitimate participants in the discourse about what journalism is, can be and
    should be"-- Provided by publisher.
Identifiers: LCCN 2019016714 (print) | LCCN 2019980604 (ebook) | ISBN
    9780745643410 (hardback) | ISBN 9780745643427 (paperback)
Subjects: LCSH: Journalism.
Classification: LCC PN4731 .D47 2019 (print) | LCC PN4731 (ebook) | DDC
    070.4--dc23
LC record available at https://lccn.loc.gov/2019016714
LC ebook record available at https://lccn.loc.gov/2019980604

Typeset in 10.5 on 12pt Sabon
by Fakenham Prepress Solutions, Fakenham, Norfolk, NR21 8NL
Printed and bound in Great Britain by CPI Group (UK) Ltd, Croydon

The publisher has used its best endeavours to ensure that the URLs for external websites referred to in this book are correct and active at the time of going to press. However, the publisher has no responsibility for the websites and can make no guarantee that a site will remain live or that the content is or will remain appropriate.

Every effort has been made to trace all copyright holders, but if any have been overlooked the publisher will be pleased to include any necessary credits in any subsequent reprint or edition.

For further information on Polity, visit our website: politybooks.com

Contents

Prologue: The Beyond Journalism Project

In the summer of 2013, Mark moved to The Netherlands after spending ten years working and living in the United States. Tamara had then just come back from maternity leave, after returning to her home country the year previous to Mark, having lived and worked in the United Kingdom for five years. Both of us assumed positions at our universities (Mark at the University of Amsterdam, Tamara at the University of Groningen) with responsibilities regarding administration, teaching, and research in journalism and media studies – at a time when both fields shifted under the influence of technological and social transformations.

Whereas changes in journalism manifest primarily in the decline (or disappearance) of local news media, with subsequent large numbers of layoffs in news organizations all over the world (and especially in overdeveloped nations), in The Netherlands we were also confronted with a new kind of energy: independent journalistic ventures such as Follow The Money (a financial-economic investigative journalism collective founded by Eric Smit, Mark Koster, and Arne van der Wal in 2009), Blendle (offering an online kiosk that sells articles from a variety of newspapers and magazines on a pay-per-article basis, started in 2012 by Marten Blankesteijn and Alexander Klöpping, and expanding to Germany and the United States in 2016), and De Correspondent (an online in-depth journalism magazine launched as a crowdfunded initiative in 2013 by Rob Wijnberg, Harald Dunnink, Sebastian Kersten, and Ernst-Jan Pfauth, opening an international division in the United States in 2018) were making headlines, both nationally and internationally. Something was brewing in our home country – a development partly inspired by the economic downturn, and greatly enabled by funding agencies such as the Dutch Journalism Fund, a government-sponsored institution offering subsidies for innovation.

Traditionally, the Dutch Journalism Fund supported legacy news media in their efforts to develop new ways of publishing news. However, in 2010 a new subsidy program was adopted (titled Persinnovatie [Innovation of the press]), redirecting its efforts to support both individual journalists and teams of journalists as well as news media organizations to take advantage of – and experiment with – new, digital opportunities. In the first five years of this program it received over 550 applications, of which 93 applications were granted with well over 10 million euro in subsidies. Approximately half of the projects were continued by the applicant after the subsidy was spent.[1]

The availability of a lot of (unemployed) journalistic talent, new sources of financial support, a growing frustration with the lack of innovation in the Dutch news media landscape (among journalists and certain segments of the public alike), as well as the emergence of charismatic and media-savvy reporters and editors such as Smit, Klöpping, and Wijnberg, cemented a path for journalism startups – admittedly, a path partially paved for them by belonging to the dominant class of journalists in The Netherlands (white, middle-class, male, well-educated, living in or near the capital). As these startups expressed a profound engagement with society, a critical attitude toward traditional newswork, as well as a commitment to the ideals of journalism, we were tremendously inspired by all this activity. We also saw the young graduates of our respective master programs in journalism (in Groningen and Amsterdam) flock to these (and other) startups, eager to have a go. All of this momentum in the startup space correlated with a growing need felt by both of us to challenge, provoke, uproot, and dislocate established theoretical frameworks and practices in journalism studies and education (and in studies on journalism and journalists within other disciplines). The developments in the pioneering startup space provided the perfect operationalization of our disciplinary concerns.

Without a clear plan other than a genuine desire to listen and find out what working in such a way was all about, we went to the Nieuwsatelier in downtown Amsterdam: the ground floor of a vacant old building in the city center housing five different media startups (and a network of associated independent journalists), managed by Follow The Money. We invited all the professionals who rented desk space in the Nieuwsatelier to dinner, as in: we brought in a caterer to cook a delicious meal for everyone involved, while Mark's students Nikki van der Westen and Fleur Launspach rigged the informal office environment with cameras and microphones. During dinner, a more than lively conversation ensued about the promises and pitfalls of startup and entre-preneurial journalism, about frustrations and excitement, about love and hate for the profession and the news industry as a whole. It was an inspiring and insightful evening that paved the way for the Beyond Journalism research project of which this book is a document.[2]

Every year since that dinner conversation (on April 11 of 2014), the empirical work continued thanks to the help of different teams of graduate students who (from 2014 onward) conducted a series of case studies of journalism startups that they found inspiring, anywhere in the world. We gradually developed a comprehensive interview protocol – loosely based on the conversations during the dinner in the Nieuwsatelier, informed by emerging research among news startups around the world. Getting access turned out to be relatively straightforward – most startups are enthusiastic to show their work and share their positive and negative experiences for others to learn from. As our students found startups all over the world – from Uganda to Colombia, from Cuba to Nepal, from Canada to Italy, from Australia to the United States – we were in need of more funding. Some initial support came from the University of Groningen as part of its Rosalind Franklin Fellowship program for Tamara and the NWO internationalization grant for the humanities, which resulted in the international research network "Journalism

Elsewhere."[3] This network support also allowed us to discuss the methodological approach and theoretical questions with the inspiring group of international researchers in meetings taking place from 2013–15.

Following this, many of our students were able to secure travel grants, for example through the Horizon Fund of the University of Amsterdam, supporting students from the humanities wishing to do research abroad. As our students were also trained journalists, they often managed to further support themselves by selling stories to news organizations about issues in the countries they visited. In 2015 we were honored to receive a joint nonresidential fellowship from the Donald W. Reynolds Journalism Institute at the University of Missouri in the United States. The financial support of this fellowship funded several case studies in the United States (and elsewhere), and enabled us to visit and spend some time at the Missouri School of Journalism to meet with students and faculty to discuss and further develop our work and ideas. In 2015, Tamara was awarded a five-year personal grant from the Dutch national research organization NWO for her research program "Entrepreneurship at Work," and in 2017 she gained additional funding from the NWO for the action research project "Exploring Journalism's Limits."[4] Both these projects contained elements that allowed us to support the research and output for the Beyond Journalism project.

By the academic year 2015–16 the first case studies were completed. Charlotte Waaijers included our dinner session in her study on Follow The Money, Shermin Chavoushi spent significant time at the fledgling De Correspondent, Lotte van Rosmalen went to California to observe the operation of InkaBinka, while Jorik Nijhuis visited Nepal to observe how Naya Pusta managed to distribute its children's television news program via discs across a country ravaged by natural disaster. Andrea Wagemans did a stellar project with Mediapart in Paris – one of the few startups we found making a profit – which led to her first scholarly journal publication (Wagemans, Witschge, and Deuze 2016), and she has continued to work on the project, transcribing and coding interviews, and is currently pursuing her PhD on innovation in journalism. Other projects that year included

Boris Lemereis's study of *360 Magazine*, Joris Zwetsloots's inspiring observation of the all-female editorial collective Bureau Boven in Amsterdam, Susan Blanken and Fleur Willemsen's coverage of The Post Online and its TPO Magazine, Heleen d'Haens's research on MMU Radio in Uganda, and Guus Ritzen and Liz Dautzenberg collaborated for their intensive fieldwork in New York while studying the six hyperlocal news startups that are part of the Brooklyn-based Corner Media Group. Luuk Ex traveled to Tehran, Iran – an area teeming with startup activity in anticipation of the market opening up after the end of economic sanctions. Under difficult circumstances, Luuk visited and profiled Jaaar (an online kiosk for all Iranian newspapers), *Peivast* (a monthly print magazine about information and communication technology), and Aparat (a video-sharing website). Amanda Brouwers and Sofie Willemsen, prior to starting their PhD research at the University of Groningen, went to the United States to research, respectively, the now-defunct *Alaska Dispatch* and the *Common Reader* (at Washington University).

In 2016–17, Alexandra van Ditmars visited Zetland in Denmark – a startup that among other activities organizes a successful annual theater performance (Zetland Live) based on their journalistic investigations throughout the year, Ronja Hijmans looked at the university-based hyperlocal The Brooklyn Ink, Hadewieg Beekman visited the documentary film venture Mediastorm (also in New York), while Renate Guitink had an inspiring time in Vancouver at the offices of the all-female investigative journalism company Discourse Media. Other cases completed were IRPI in Italy by Milou van der Zwan, Sophie Frankenmolen and Evelien Veldboom's study of Code4SA in Johannesburg (South Africa), and a detailed profile of La Silla Vacía in Colombia by Tessa Colen.

During the next academic year, 2017–18, we used all the data from these thesis projects coupled with our own projects (such as Mark's involvement with the international New Beats study, investigating what happens to journalists after they have been laid off) to conduct a comparative case study, and started the writing process for this book. At the same time, a new student cohort continued the work, shifting focus to an emerging trend of legacy news organizations who, noticing the energy and innovative potential of startup culture, create spaces within their companies for "intrapreneurial" teams of motivated reporters and editors – often supplemented with other professionals, including data analysts, social media experts, and representatives from marketing departments. Although the data from these studies could not be included in the formal analysis in our book, we want to acknowledge the work of the students involved, as their experiences and insights certainly contributed to our work. Livia Benders studied the Digital Storytelling Initiative (DSI) at the ABC in Australia, Wisanne van 't Zelfde looked at Dag6 (an online joint venture between a Dutch national newspaper and a public broadcaster), and Marit Willemsen observed the operations of the MediaLab, part of Dutch public broadcasting organization VPRO. The reporters and editors at both the MediaLab and the DSI found out they were being shut down during the time of our investigation, providing more testament to the precariousness of beyond journalism – within as much as outside of legacy institutions. At the time of writing, the work still continues, with independent journalism cases under investigation in Argentina (Revista Anfibia), Spain (El Diario), Cuba (PostData), and Belgium (Apache).

The project and this book can be considered to be a personal passion project for us. It is a way to operationalize our excitement about everything that is possible under the umbrella concept of "journalism" as much as it is a way to bypass or at least alleviate the frustration all too often found in journalism studies about the various problems legacy news organizations face. We wanted to focus on the people driving journalism forward, the professionals who are opening up the field while being committed to both personal motivation and professional and public ideals: making journalism content that matters, whether on a small scale informing individuals, or at societal level, responding to and affecting public issues.

Our aim throughout is to tell new stories that open our concept of what journalism is (or should be), and what journalism is for. To further our aim to tell the stories from the heart of the startup journalists, we have added in-depth contextual narratives, inserted as boxes in the empirical chapters. For this, we are deeply indebted to Andrea

Wagemans, who has – as she has done for all the quotes used in this book – mined the data. We hope these boxes engage the reader, and add yet another way of letting the startups speak for themselves. We also acknowledge the invaluable work of Sofie Willemsen (as well as the anonymous reviewers of our initial manuscript), who provided expert comments and feedback on the manuscript. Through telling stories of startups we hope to do justice to the variety of actors; the multitude of forms, content, and audiences of those startups; and the scope of their excitement, drive, struggle, and ambition to make for what they feel is a better journalism.

Introduction: What Is Journalism (Studies)?

What is journalism for? The starting point of this book is that journalism holds great potential to further the imagination, and performs a variety of functions (beyond informing citizens) that are necessary for society to thrive. We see, however, that in realigning itself to fit the changing social, technological, and political landscape, journalism as a profession, as well as news as an industry, struggles to transform itself. This is where journalism *studies* should come in, as a scholarly endeavor that assists and inspires the field to self-assess, move forward, and innovate. It is our contention that journalism studies – even before it became an established field at the dawn of the twenty-first century – furthered a rather narrow picture of the profession and its performance and role in society, thereby reifying its internal (industrial) operations, and limiting its creative potential.

Beyond journalism (studies)

In its eagerness both to prepare students for jobs in the news industry and to understand and explain journalism's functioning in (the service of) democratic societies (while consistently framing this function as being under threat, thereby collapsing concerns about news as an industry with journalism as a profession), journalism studies and education have constructed a theoretical framework that considers the profession in terms of its more or less consensual news values, dominant frames, routinized operations, gatekeeping functions, and industrial arrangements. This is not to say scholars of journalism have not studied nonmainstream, oppositional, grassroots, or any other kind of nontraditional form of journalism in the past. Such "journalisms," however, were generally reined in and tamed in theoretical frameworks emphasizing inside/outside binaries – for example, between mainstream and alternative journalism, between hard versus soft news, or between information and entertainment functions of the press. In doing so, a certain way of doing (and thinking about) journalism has prevailed – providing a benchmark of sorts.

At the same time, when journalism educators, students, and researchers talk about journalism, they cannot help but recognize the enormous diversity of the field. Professionals, amateurs, and hybrid variations of such identities, many institutions, many technologies, are all involved in the production of journalism across diverse channels and platforms. With so many actors involved of so many types, our conceptualizations of journalism as a single (more or less consensual) entity are challenged. When we revert to the same old dualisms, we risk explaining this complexity away, reflexively suggesting there is a *core* to the profession that continually reflects on itself vis-à-vis the developments in and challenges of the *periphery*, in a continuous circling of the wagons to keep truly original, edgy, pioneering, creative, nonformulaic, nontraditional ways of newsgathering, storytelling, and audience engagement at the perimeter. In keeping with this center/periphery distinction, anything not fitting preconceived notions of coherence is labeled as diverse, complex, or hybridized. Such approach does not acknowledge the messiness intrinsic to the object of study, a messiness amplified and accelerated by changes in working conditions, in information and communication technologies, and challenges to established business models: "we need to be ready to see the conceptual mess that we made through neatly fitting everything in categories that never quite fit" (Witschge et al. 2019: 657).

The conceptual and theoretical building blocks of journalism studies, news values, framing and agenda setting, and occupational ideology can all be considered examples of routines, conventions, and formulas that developed (and continue to develop) – arising out of conversations in workplaces, debates in newsrooms, choices by individuals in a variety of circumstances. That is, these concepts and theories are continually contingent on practices. The ongoing and dynamic discursive construction of journalism as an idea as well as a praxis tends to be dictated by casuistry (rather than a strict principle-based approach) and *everydayness*. In Heideggerian (1927) terms, everydayness in journalism manifests in journalists' generally pragmatic way of engaging the daily challenges of newswork. Lefebvre's (1987) use of the concept of everydayness is relevant as well: how those engagements over time have a tendency to become repetitive, routinized, even monotonous – quite possibly soon to be replaced by automation and robot (or algorithmic) journalism (Carlson 2015).

Although this would suggest that one could equate "journalism" with the sum of routines, conventions, and formulas emerging from the newsroom-centric construction of the profession, we want to pinpoint and highlight all the other ways of understanding and doing journalism, being a journalist, that aren't necessarily "peripheral" or even exceptional but simply also make up the essence of the profession. It can be argued that well-established patterned behaviors are what students and scholars may have focused on, and they may be what journalism education is structured around. Such behaviors may be what the major news institutions use to standardize work. In everyday practices, though, there is always what Robert Chia and Robin Holt call "wayfinding," which they characterize "not as a plotted sequence of static positions but as the coming-into-sight and passing-out-of-sight of various contoured and textured aspects of the environment" (2009: 163). We run the risk of ignoring the many opportunistic, unplanned, improvised, intimate, and curious acts that make up journalism if we consistently attempt to solidify these into the well-worn concepts of our handbooks and canonical works (Chia and Holt label the models, maps, and classifications as the "navigational" behavior of professionals in organizations). Accessing practices through the lens of wayfinding underscores how institutional journalism is becoming a different place. Internally these institutions are reshuffling, being repopulated by a wide variety of new actors – often with only temporary assignments, working on a per-project basis. Journalism is increasingly practiced outside of such institutions. It is crucial to expand upon the exclusivity of journalism studies and education, to move beyond binaries, and seek out the stories and conversations of journalists elsewhere.

The navigational (Chia and Holt 2009) ties that bind journalism are the ones most efficiently theorized by the field of journalism studies, and consist of what journalists (and academics) know and understand to be the cornerstones of the profession: role perceptions and news values, ways of framing information that assist audiences to make sense of (particularly) the world of politics and the economy, and its purpose and corresponding privileged position in democratic society (Hanitzsch and Vos 2017). The theory and research falls short in that it conceptualizes these ties as necessarily operationally coupled with the structure of the news outlets and media organizations as an industry, and designates the institutional arrangement of news as work. Second, it does not allow enough space for understanding the many ways that journalistic practices and self-understandings defy these conceptualizations. In this book we thus call for acknowledging how our theoretical frameworks and empirical analyses exclude a great number of the practices, emotions, values, and definitions currently constituting journalism. We hope to contribute to the telling of multiple and multiperspectival (Gans 2011) stories about journalism so that we can contribute to the development of definitions and research frameworks that "do not foreclose on rearrangements suggested by new forms of social and natural knowledge" (Bowker and Star quoted in Timmermans 2015: 7).

Throughout its history, the general notion or idea of journalism has stayed more or less the same. Its core values and ideals remain intact. Its commitment to public service, truth-seeking, and providing information on the basis of professional and independent verification has been presumed and widely affirmed. In other words: when looking at journalism writ large, the tendency to see coherence is strong. When one switches to individual journalists – when the unit of analysis becomes what newsworkers do and under what conditions they do it – a messy reality emerges. Scholars such as Thomas Hanitzsch and Tim Vos acknowledge how the discussion about "what journalism is" changes when we take into account the profound and dramatic changes in journalists' working environments. The question remains of how this could be, given the cognitive consensus about journalism and the continual "testing" of more or less new journalisms vis-à-vis a supposed core.

What is interesting (and what needs to be challenged) is not so much the question of what journalism is but how it has so successfully remained similar in the context of continuous internal and external transformations, changes, challenges, evolutions, and revolutions. It is revealing how the scholarly (and all too human) proclivity for closure and coherence has preferred to conflate the various levels of analysis when making sense of media work. This is most explicitly and famously articulated in several models: John Dimmick and Philip Coit's (1982) taxonomy of mass media decision-making, Armin Scholl and Siegfried Weischenberg's (1998) onion model, and Stephen Reese and Pamela Shoemaker's (2016) hierarchy-of-influences framework. Instead of working through how the various stages of newswork change under individualized, fragmented, networked, and altogether precarious conditions, as educators and researchers we have tended to focus on consistency across levels, proclaiming more or less "universal" theories of journalism, its culture, and its role conceptions. In doing so, we have accepted explanations of newswork that assume journalists get their ideas of who they are and what they are (supposed to be) doing largely through occupational socialization and occupational context, leading to homogeneous understandings of what journalism is.

Whereas influential, multinational comparative research projects such as Worlds of Journalism (worldsofjournalism. org) and Journalistic Role Performance (journalisticper-formance.org) started out with universalist ambitions, their most recent reports and publications suggest otherwise, emphasizing "multilayered hybridization in journalistic cultures" (Mellado et al. 2017: 961) and a world populated by a rich diversity of journalistic cultures (Hanitzsch et al. 2019). What these remarkable projects do not do, however, is to offer an explanation for all this diversity, hybridity, and complexity.

To provide insight into the many variations, seemingly contradictory definitions, activities, values, and aims that all exist under the banner of journalism, we suggest turning our attention to the affective dimension of news as work, of journalism as a profession. This affective dimension points to the strong affiliation that practitioners have to ideals of journalism, irrespective of the medium they produce for, their contract, or type of working arrangement. They can be quite critical of management, of industry, even of specific routines and practices associated with newswork – but they somehow see such criticisms as separate from their loyalty to – their passion for, even – the notion of doing journalistic work as a professional. In writing this book we have seen this most clearly among those who invent "journalism" from the ground up, sticking to quite traditional notions of newswork while making entire new companies, ventures, and collectives work. In this context legacy news organizations and newsrooms – while valuable and important – can also be a major distraction from reflecting on what exactly is (or also is) journalism. Once inside, the relative stability of the institutional setting absolves most journalists from actively questioning who they are, why they are doing what they are doing, and who they are doing it for. Consistently, those journalists operating in emerging or otherwise peripheral areas of the profession are challenged to be more reflective, deliberate, and articulate about what it is that they are doing. Those working on the inside, within the confines of the newsroom, have their positions governed by the institutional authority of their employer, and, though they are certainly involved in boundary work, can be considered to be less challenged to continuously legitimate what it is they are doing. This attitude is something Ellen Ullman once documented as the inherent blindness of being "close to the machine" (1997) – the machine in our case being the core of institutionalized newswork.

The notion of journalism as a form of affective labor is not new, yet remains underarticulated (Beckett and Deuze 2016; Siapera 2019; Cantillon and Baker 2019). The affective nature of newswork gets expressed in the need for reporters to regulate and moderate their emotions and emotional life in order to "make it work" as journalists (for example, to always be amenable and pleasant to work with, to empathize with interviewees and assignment editors, at times to process the trauma of victims or witnesses to accidents and attacks, to nurture relationships with online and offline communities). As an extreme form of affect, journalism can also be seen as a passion project for many involved, at times accepting (or shrugging off) poor working conditions in order to keep doing what one loves doing.

In our project, we aim to go beyond journalism in that our studies articulate the field with those who strike out on their own, while deliberately focusing on the affective dimensions of journalism. The startup journalists we interviewed and observed are not alone in what they do: they are reporters and editors setting up new journalistic entities, starting editorial collectives, building a news business from the ground up, all over the world, across distinctly different journalism traditions and news cultures. In all these instances of entrepreneurial activity and bottom-up initiatives, we looked for the different notions and definitions of what journalism could be, what it means to be a journalist under these conditions, and what issues confront the contemporary journalist operating outside of the institutionalized contours of legacy news organizations.

This book is personal, in the cases and professionals it documents and in our focus on the stories of the heart, as well as in our motivations. Mark is beyond journalism: this is the last major work he will do in relation to journalism. Or so he says. Tamara thinks he is beyond *journalism studies*, needing to break free of the (perceived) regime of journalism scholars, which seems to leave little space for creative thinking (for a critique of the paradigm see, for instance, Josephi 2013; Zelizer 2013). Any academic work is a balance between "personal creative passion and willingness to submit to tradition and discipline" as Michael Polanyi (1998: 40) puts it. To have our work be recognized as academic work, we play by certain rules. But, as we argue in this book, journalism studies oftentimes can be too limited in scope, resulting in a narrow conceptualization of journalism as a fourth estate (with a subsequent primary focus on national politics and the economy), operated in newsrooms of legacy media institutions, serving a relatively silent and amorphous citizenry. Where Mark experiences a sense of frustration with the recurring debates reinforcing the dogma of the field, the industry, and the profession, and advocates a strategic bypassing of journalism in order to break free, Tamara sees tactical potential through her multiple engagements with the field "elsewhere" and outside the boundaries of established methodological and practical frameworks, and challenges to established ways of seeing (and doing) things.

This then is one of the main aims of the book: to both strategically and tactically affect journalism studies and education, and through that help facilitate more inclusive, diverse, and creative journalism practices. This book can be considered to be both a manifesto and an empirical description of part of the field of journalism. We aim to get journalism studies beyond journalism studies by showing how journalism is beyond (what we have predominantly defined as) journalism. Moving beyond does not – cannot – entail a full divorce from what came before. That which we counter grows from the same intellectual soil that we come from (Ortega y Gasset 1967: 73–4). As José Ortega y Gasset (1967: 74) points out, any creative thought is "shaped in opposition to some other thought, which we believe erroneous, fallacious, and needful of correction." So, that which we argue against in this book is what at this "particular moment looms above our soil" for us, but our roots are from the same soil, and this book is as much homage to as critique of the very field that we grew up in. And we know that we keep it alive by writing this book as well: as Ortega y Gasset goes on to say, the "adversary is never an ineffectual past: it is always contemporary and seemingly vestigial." We hope to add as much as transform, and in doing so our actions as academics mirror those of the journalists profiled in this book, especially their hopes and aspirations to both contribute to as well as change journalism.

Telling new stories

Our aim then is not to erase our "adversary"; it is not even to combat it. Our aim is to complement and impact the field through telling stories – stories that are somewhat different from those told in mainstream journalism studies not only because of our object of study, our focus on the affective nature of newswork, but also in terms of style. As pointed out by Roberta Štěpánková (2015: 313), we may ask at some point in our academic lives: "Is my storytelling right?" As she reminds us: "there are no 'correct' stories, just multiple stories." This is our attempt to be part of a growing movement among scholars as well as practitioners to make space for different kinds of stories.

We do so by focusing on a particular group of journalists: journalists who are involved in starting up (or who are in the process of setting up) small news companies outside the legacy media. These startup journalists can be seen as pioneers in the field. Pioneering communities are, in Andreas Hepp's terms, "experimental groupings related to new forms of media-technology-related change and collectivity formation" (2016: 920). Pioneering communities "have a sense of mission" and have "a sense that they are at the 'forefront' of a media-related transformation of society as a whole" (Hepp 2016: 924–5). This is very much the case with the startup journalists and organizational contexts we have visited. These newsworkers are keenly aware of the role that they play, not only in society, but also in defining what journalism is as it charts new territory in the twenty-first century. This reflexivity is also something that Hepp refers to as characteristic of pioneering communities, "since they are engaged in a continual process of interpretation of themselves" (2016: 927). Furthermore, the spaces and places our cases use to facilitate their work are varied, constituting a range of pioneering and innovative practices. Oscar Westlund and Seth Lewis (2014) rightly consider "agents of media innovation" not just the individual professionals and communities involved, but also the role technologies, working environments, and other nonhuman actors play. By focusing on this group of journalists and their working arrangements and environments, we are able to add valuable stories of those in the field who are looking to contribute to the conceptualization of what journalism is. Moreover, in our analysis we are focusing on those stories and narratives that attest to the affective nature of the profession, providing much-needed emotional context for the question how these pioneers make it work on their own.

Our project recognizes an overall historical phase, where journalism worldwide is in a process of becoming a different kind of industry: less reliant on legacy news organizations, producing a great variety of contents and services, published across multiple platforms by practitioners in all kinds of formal and informal ways. This phase roughly coincides with the rise of new technologies (notably internet, smartphones, and various forms of automation), the shift of nation-based politics toward more complex supranational relations (as well as its return under the guise of populism), and a rapid glocalization of social, cultural, and economic affairs. The news industry, in response to such changes and challenges, has generally sought answers in consolidating its core business and streamlining existing operations. This meant laying off employees (including many journalists) and cutting budgets. The budgets for exploratory innovation projects, specialized beats (such as science reporting), and a range of correspondents were all trimmed. Journalism was once mostly organized in formal institutions where contracted laborers would produce content under informal yet highly structured working conditions generally arranged within the physical environment of a newsroom. Today the lived experience of professional journalists is much more precarious, fragmented, and networked.

Our starting point is that journalism is much more than its traditional definition: an activity operationally coupled with institutions of newswork. The boundaries between journalism and other forms of public communication – public relations, marketing, and corporate communication to the (generally unpaid) practices of mass self-communication online (via weblogs, videoblogs and podcasts, or simply through posts on social media) – are porous and often meaningless, particularly for media users. The digital environment has blurred the once clear distinction between the various phases of the news production process – including the gathering, verifying, reporting, editing, designing, distributing, publicizing, and promoting of information. This digital environment also sees a disruption of the unity of production, content, and distribution within each separate medium in favor of the development of new storytelling formats across multiple media (e.g. transmedia), new ways of delivering the news (increasingly via mobile and social media), and most significantly new ways of being a journalist. All of these developments require us to tell new stories about journalism: what it is, how it can be practiced, and what roles it plays in communities.

With Joep Cornelissen (2017: 369), we argue that any field of studies is generally "best served by a combination of styles of theorizing and the different explanatory programmes associated with them, so that different questions get asked and different modes of knowing sit alongside each other in a complementary fashion." Both of us feel that the dominant tools of researching and telling stories in journalism studies are too restricted. Content analyses of high-profile national newspapers (and sometimes television newscasts) and surveys among journalists working in the newsrooms of legacy media organizations tell part of the story. Dominant theories such as news values, framing and agenda-setting, and journalism professionalization are necessary but limited. We question the lack of inclusivity of the diversity of voices heard in the field – as local, community, grassroots, minority, and independent media organizations tend to be all too often ignored in both journalism studies and education. The socialization effect of the dominant ways of thinking and writing about our object of study may mean that "particular ways of knowing" become suppressed (Cornelissen 2017: 370). The corresponding homogeneity in the field "has the potential to undermine variety, novelty, and innovation in research" (Corbett et al. 2014: 4). Although this homogenization can have benefits, providing a common ground for engaging in academic discussion of issues across diverse regions, for example, this move to conformity also has the potential to undermine creativity and the widest possible range of insights.

This is not to say there is no diversity in journalism studies. In fact, quite the opposite could be argued: the field has proliferated, opening up plentiful ways to investigate, theorize, and rethink journalism. Interestingly, the response to this diversification has largely been to test the merits of any novel or innovative approach against the dominant model and mode of journalism, which in effect colonized the intervention, making it subject to the rules established at the center.

Our aim is to tell new stories, and expand our storytelling format (what we choose to tell our stories about) as well as what we understand journalism to be. Much like William Gartner's ambition for organization studies, we are not interested in providing a "one best way" model for journalism, as we are much more interested in highlighting the "need for mid-range theories that reflect contingent relationships" (1993: 236). Like Gartner, we are interested in specificities rather than generalities in the field at this stage. The field tends to understand journalism through a framework that suggests a homogenous entity as the object of study (or as an internally consistent reference point). We would like to consider the differences that truly make a difference, and recognize new or emerging voices as legitimate participants in setting the discourse about what journalism is, can, and should be.

The state of the field

Journalism has enjoyed a rich and relatively stable history of professionalization. This has contributed to a more or less consensual notion of its core values and ideals, often grounded in the practices and routines of newswork as organized within legacy media organizations, and shared among journalists and the public alike (Karlsson and Clerwall 2018). Scholars coming from a variety of disciplines have theorized this history, forming a relatively consistent body of knowledge codified in national and international handbooks and canonical readers. However, recent work and analysis suggests that the supposed core of journalism, as well as the assumed consistency of the inner workings of news organizations, are problematic starting points for journalism studies. In this project we challenge the operational coupling of journalism's occupational ideology, professional culture, and sedimentation in routines and organizational structures (the newsroom) in the context of its reconfiguration as an increasingly *post-industrial*, *entrepreneurial*, and *atypical* way of working and of being at work.[1] We aim to outline a way beyond individualist and institutionalist approaches to do justice to the current complex transformation of the profession. We propose a framework to bring together these approaches in a dialectical attempt to move through and *beyond* journalism as it has traditionally been conceptualized and practiced, allowing for a broader definition and understanding of the myriad practices that make up journalism.

Journalism, as a profession, has enjoyed a long and stable development in most countries around the world. Whether working under conditions of censorship, pressures of nation-building, or with expectations of providing a society with social cement, journalism is widely recognized and seen as a set of values, principles, and practices enacted in different ways and settings with a "sense of wholeness and seamlessness" (Hallin 1992: 14) around the world. Similarly, the field of journalism studies – the scholarly pursuit of knowledge about journalism – developed alongside its object into an increasingly sophisticated and consensual body of knowledge, range of research methodologies, and theoretical developments. This focus on coherence and consensus does not do justice to the insight that journalism is more than a neat sum of its parts, and to the need to accommodate a more dynamic and indeed unruly consideration of the profession. Journalism is transitioning from a coherent industry (largely organized around sedimented practices and ways of working) to a highly varied arrangement of journalistic practices and a diverse range of opportunities to be a journalist.

Scholars and educators tend to respond to this shift in two ways. One is to rally the troops, close ranks, and put significant effort in bringing coherence and stability (back) to the field. This gets established by producing impressive handbooks, canonical anthologies, readers, and companion volumes (and corresponding special issues of scholarly journals and conferences). Empirical approaches in this tradition center on comprehensive surveys and content analyses of journalists and journalism based on narrow definitions of the news industry offering conclusions about what journalism is and who journalists are (see Willnat, Weaver, and Choi 2013; Hanitzsch et al. 2011; Hellmueller and Mellado 2015).

A second trend in the field is to dive, head first, into the chaos. This proves to be an often exciting and bewildering experience, leading to a wide variety of studies and conceptualizations of journalism in a post-industrial era, often featuring particularistic work on emerging and more or less innovative genres, formats, and types of journalism. Theoretically, journalism research in this context enthusiastically explores the boundaries of the field (Carlson and Lewis 2015), or shows through a surge in ethnographic fieldwork how even the traditional "inside" of the profession – the newsroom – is not as coherent as it is generally made out to be (Anderson 2011). Conceptually, such work can be considered to be walking in the footsteps of Colin Sparks's much earlier realization, that "from every point of view it seems sensible to adopt a more catholic definition of journalism and of the scope of the press" (1991: 66). The point is that the core functions and roles of journalism are practiced in so many different ways and places, that conventional distinctions (such as between newspapers and magazines, online and offline, inside or outside of the traditional newsroom) quite simply fail to recognize "one of the fundamental contemporary realities of the press and the actual dynamic of its development" (Sparks 1991: 66). Sparks's notion of a "catholic" definition – a definition that includes a wide variety of practices – asks us to be more inclusive when it comes to allowing a myriad of practices, genres, and forms to be considered when defining (as well as studying and doing) journalism.

In this intervention we bring together these approaches to move *beyond* journalism, allowing for not so much a redefinition but a more inclusive appreciation and understanding of the field that in turn grounds the multiple case study approach in our work for this book. In doing so, our work sides with a growing number of interventions in the field to open up and consider complexity and hybridity; it aims to expand our toolkit to make sense of journalism and its role in society.

Structure of this book

As Montuori (2003: 543) notes about writing in the academic genre, it is "easier to leave all the personal, ambiguous, contextual material out. It is ultimately easier, I believe, to present just the context of justification, and leave out the messy context of discovery – or creation." Indeed, both of us have found it a "tremendous creative challenge to be more transparent, to be more fully present" (ibid.) in this work, and though we both embrace this, what you will find here is only a partial answer to this challenge. We consider this book as a stepping-stone toward a more transparent, personal, and creative way of researching and writing about our field of study.

In the first part of the book, on the becoming of journalism, we critically interrogate the normative expectations of what journalism should be and do according to dominant conceptualizations of the profession. Newsrooms and newswork are part of a profession that can best be seen as a self-organizing social system through which shifting coalitions of participants are linked, and that is interdependent with a variety of other systems – such as sales, marketing, design, programming and coding, publishing and distribution services – in terms of its business models as well as its practices (consider, for example, emerging genres such as branded content, native advertising, automated journalism, and news aggregation).

It is also a field with a distinct *materiality of praxis* (Sartre 1976: 79) – what journalism is and what journalists do cannot be meaningfully separated from their material context (such as physical workspaces, hardware and software, and technological affordances).

From this broad perspective, we outline how journalism is not nearly as consistent nor homogeneous as it is made out to be, and focus instead on providing stories of journalism that show the multiple, seemingly contradictory (self-) understandings, activities, values, and emotions that are part of the professional practice of journalism. In the subsequent chapters we operationalize this approach by focusing on those reporters, editors, and associated staffers who make up the countless startups, new media companies, editorial collectives, and other forms of small enterprises that are emerging all over the world. These are journalists who, as pioneer communities, give shape to the profession in all kinds of ways, deliberately and self-reflexively, a process that we document with a sense of wonder. How do they make it work, what does it take to strike out on your own like that, what does journalism mean to them, and what is the price they pay for their endeavors?

There is no neat summary and conclusion at the end of this book. We do not have a list of tips and tricks for how to be successful as a news startup and a journalism entrepreneur. We have opted to focus on particularity rather than imposing some kind of consistency or uniformity onto the data, onto our subjects. Throughout the book we have added short vignettes highlighting and profiling specific initiatives and people that we found inspiring or remarkable. These are people who made us think twice before labeling them in order to fit some preconceived notion of being a journalist or an entrepreneur. Ultimately, we hope the Beyond Journalism project, as initially outlined in this book, opens up fruitful ways of further exploration. Journalism is not on its way out, nor is it simply morphing into something else – it is being reimagined and creatively and passionately practiced in lots of different ways, and our work aspires to provide access to that process and these practices.

1

The Becoming of Journalism

Students and scholars coming from a wide variety of disciplines have researched and theorized journalism, resulting in a more or less coherent conceptualization of what journalism is (Zelizer 2004) and could be (Zelizer 2016). Here, our argument is that in treating journalism predominantly as a stable object, journalism studies cannot deal with the complexity – the continuous change and state of becoming in the field – beyond simply testing whatever is considered to be new against the presupposed core of the profession and industry. Ultimately, focusing our exploration on the ongoing transformation and fragmentation of journalism, we need to view journalism as a moving object, as a process, as something that is continuously constituted as it is practiced. In other words: we need to ask *how journalism is becoming*, rather than *what journalism is*. Journalism theory has to be benchmarked by a critical assessment of the role, work, and milieu of individual journalists, while recognizing the object of study – journalism – as dynamic: requiring an ontology of becoming rather than of being (Chia 1995). With Robert Chia, we propose a perspective on journalism that privileges "reality as a processual, heterogeneous and emergent configuration of relations" (ibid.: 594).

To set up our exploration, and to provide the context relevant to understanding both journalism practice and journalism studies, we first discuss the way in which journalism has predominantly been defined. We consider major trends that question the continued adequacy of dominant conceptualizations, and we argue that it is not just a matter of finding a better definition, however inclusive it would be. We ask instead that we apply our creative attention to the way in which we theorize (and thus research and report on) journalism. The criteria that allow us to define journalism are not the only aspect of this that needs change. Shifting practices means we need theories of journalism that are defined by activities and discourses. To define journalism in terms of *places*, *people* and *products* is too reductive, we argue.

The general approach to understanding, studying, teaching, and practicing journalism articulates the profession with a specific occupational ideology as well as specific values and culture. Journalists tend to benchmark their actions and attitudes self-referentially using ideal-typical standards, seeing themselves as providing a public service; being objective, fair, and (therefore) trustworthy; working autonomously; committed to an operational logic of actuality and speed (preeminent in concepts such as reporting on breaking news, getting the story first); and having a social responsibility and ethical sensibility (Deuze 2005). This conceptualization of journalism as an ideology – or what Jay Rosen alternatively labels as "pressthink"[1] – is still strong within the field today, and endures even in the midst of profound changes and challenges to the profession.

Through the occupational ideology of journalism, we can define the field from the inside out, helping us to understand how the profession makes sense of itself. External definitions of journalism tend to be more functional and instrumental, where the profession is considered to provide a particular function for (democratic) society, "informing citizens in a way that enables them to act as citizens" (Costera-Meijer 2001: 13). Seen from such a function-specific perspective, journalism gets identified as distinct from other media professions (such as public relations) "as a societal system providing society with fact-based, relevant and current information" (Görke and Scholl 2007: 651). Democratic theories of the profession attribute seminal status to it, as Michael Schudson, for example, defines journalism as "the business or practice of producing and disseminating information about contemporary affairs of general public interest and importance" (2003: 11). Schudson sees journalism in terms of what it "can do for democracy" (2008: 11): journalism is supposed to inform, investigate, analyze, mobilize, provide multiple perspectives and a public forum, and publicize representative democracy.

From this point of departure, the literature diverges, one strand embracing universalist notions of journalism, showing how it gives meaning to itself in its culture – where culture is seen as the way in which a particular group (say, journalists working at a specific project or within a particular context, such as a newsroom, a medium, a country or region) works and how group members make sense of this. Thomas Hanitzsch (2007) defined this "universal" culture of journalism as constituted by its institutional role in society, its epistemology, and its ethical ideology. Surveys of (and interviews with) journalists, almost always sampled from within legacy news organizations, fuel such claims by asking journalists a set of standardized questions about role perceptions and professional values. They suggest consensus and add coherence to a global journalism that is as aspirational as it is universal among working journalists (Löffelholz and Weaver 2008; Weaver and Willnat 2012).

There is also much critical debate among newsworkers as well as journalism students and scholars about an assumed homogeneity of the profession. The discussion on the elements of journalism (Kovach and Rosenstiel 2014) tends to assume a stable core of news values and professional standards. This is a problematic assumption in the case of journalism, as the reference to a consensual core (of "elements") excludes marginalized and minority voices, tends to ignore a wide variety of practices and forms of journalism, and generally inserts a particular hierarchy in notions of what journalism is or could be.

Generally lacking formal boundaries and therefore relying on communication about itself to define and validate its privileged position in society, journalism recently has been reconceptualized in terms of its continuous *boundary work*, consisting of "efforts to establish and enlarge the limits of one domain's institutional authority relative to outsiders, thus creating social boundaries that yield greater cultural and material resources for insiders" (Lewis 2012: 841). Research among journalists working for organizations, companies, or units within mainstream news media as well as those on the sidelines shows how they engage repeatedly in boundary work, intensely debating what journalism is and who can be considered to be a ("real") journalist – and that such discussions have always been intrinsic to the profession and its associated practices (Lewis and Carlson 2015).

Even journalism's assumed significance for the functioning of democracies has come under serious scrutiny. Beate Josephi argues that such a corollary is "too limiting and distorting a lens through which journalism can be viewed in the 21st century" (2013: 445). Barbie Zelizer (2013: 469–70) critiques the type of scholarship that has resulted from incessantly linking journalism and democracy: "many existing discussions of journalism have become insular, static, exclusionary, marginalizing, disconnected, elitist, unrepresentative and historically and geographically myopic." Regardless of the colorful variety of journalistic forms and functions existing and emerging in the world, much of journalism scholarship has tended to shield its eyes from this blinding light of diversity – instead arguing for unification. The consolidation of journalism studies in the literature mainly serves the modern project of bringing an inherently unruly object under control (Steensen and Ahva 2015: 3). It is crucial to recognize that the supposed core of journalism as well as the assumed consistency of the inner workings of news organizations is anything but consensual, nor is it necessarily the norm. At the same time, it would be a mistake to assume that the types of journalism emerging inside and alongside legacy news organizations are necessarily different or oppositional to the core values, ideals, and practices of the profession.

Beyond definitions?

The developments currently transpiring in journalism are not new, or necessarily solely inspired by contemporary technological advances. In his influential 1996 paper titled "Beyond

Journalism" (on which we base the title of our book, with his kind permission), Dutch media policy scholar Jo Bardoel advocated that, mainly because of audience fragmentation, increased technological dependency, empowered users through interactivity, and disintermediation, two types of professional journalism would have to evolve: *orientating* and *instrumental* journalism (1996: 296–7). In his view, orientating journalism would provide a general public with general orientation (background, commentary, explanation), whereas instrumental journalism offers functional, specialized information to interested audiences or customers.

In a 2003 update to Bardoel's work, Mark modeled a potential future for journalism to include two more types of journalism: *monitorial* journalism and *dialogical* journalism (Deuze 2003). Monitorial journalism would offer audiences a chance to ask journalists questions and participate in directing reporters' efforts toward certain topics to be covered. This kind of journalism assumes that while people may not always be engaged with or committed to follow the news, sometimes people can be alerted and mobilized around specific issues in relation to which they can turn to the experts in news organizations (who would need to be attuned to those audiences' interests). In dialogical journalism, the professional goal would be to promote public debate by including people in all aspects of the production of news stories, up to and including forms of so-called citizen reporting (Deuze 2003: 216–21). In an update to this analysis, Juho Ruotsalainen (2018) found evidence for all four types of journalism, suggesting that the historical trajectory of transformations in journalism tends toward more dialogical and instrumental journalisms.

Although it is safe to say that elements of all these kinds of journalism are indeed found in present-day practices and strategies of news media, these analyses suffer from a major problem that we aim to address in this book: none of the authors were willing to assume at the time that what could be considered to be "professional journalism" could exist anywhere but in the hallways and corridors of legacy news media institutions, as represented by the contours of newsrooms and the reporters and editors working for such institutions. Such an omission is problematic on both theoretical as well as practical grounds. We quite simply cannot explain journalism (anymore) by just looking at established news media companies – or limit our understanding of what goes on within such institutions to the purview of pressthink.

First, digital technologies have affected the field. A myriad of news providers, platforms, aggregators, and distributors both inside and outside of the traditional industrial shell have gained prominent power – most notably new digital intermediaries such as Facebook and Google. Second, the ongoing integration of editorial, marketing, and management at most news organizations today furthermore blurs who counts as a journalist in such work contexts, as job titles and descriptions (like technical support staff, copy editors, ombudsmen and reader representatives, designers, producers, videographers, community managers, social media moderators, curators, engagement editors, content managers, coders, and programmers) proliferate. Third, journalists are finding work in increasingly diverse fields of enterprise, for example by working as a reporter for both commercial and nonprofit entities (including marketing and advertising agencies having companies as clients that demand investigative reporting as part of their communication strategy to stakeholders, and even local governments who hire journalists to cover town hall meetings in the absence of regular news coverage), forming editorial collectives (generally cross-subsidizing revenue streams by combining journalistic work with providing a host of related services such as copy editing, report writing, and content curation), or beginning journalistic startups.

Journalism increasingly takes place and shape elsewhere: at the edges and outside of traditional institutions, in new organizational settings, and also in alternative places inside of legacy media. Beyond such fairly straightforward observations about the complex, fragmented, and diverse nature of what constitutes journalism as a profession, we need to carefully reconsider journalism theoretically as well. A seminal role in providing the collective memory and social cement of societies is generally attributed to journalism by academics and by journalists themselves, guided by "the modernist bias of its official self-presentation" (Zelizer 2004: 112). John Hartley additionally notes how professionally produced news can be seen as "the sense-making practice of modernity" (1996: 32), contributing to a view of journalism as essential to constituting and maintaining social order and democracy itself. Modern journalism has consistently defined and legitimized itself as such, claiming to provide a public service regarding the democratic state. How are we to appropriately understand and classify journalism, however, when it is produced in service to a marketing strategy (as is generally the case with so-called native advertising or branded content), or as part of someone's weblog or vlog, or by a well-meaning citizen on a hyperlocal news website, or as part of an initiative by an international nongovernmental organization to raise awareness about a particular issue? If we acknowledge that journalism comes in many shapes and sizes and serves many purposes across all media, produced by people in a variety of (semi-) professional contexts, how is democracy and the ideal of an informed citizenry served by all these different journalisms, by this wide variety of actors?

A modernist focus on journalism tends to depart from two key assumptions: first, that journalism as a profession is important, that it has a public function and is correspondingly a significant influence when it comes to politics, the economy, public opinion, and culture. Second, that such a function is best served by established news institutions in society who commit themselves to providing people with truthful and trustworthy news. Given the profound changes to the arrangement and organization of newswork and the subsequent redistribution of journalism as a profession across a widening range of professionals, places, and platforms, a more liquid modern (Bauman 2000) definition of journalism can be added – not as an institution in society but rather as a range of practices, norms, and values that can exist and function beyond such institutions.

In this scenario, what could be seen to demarcate journalism from other activities and professions are the notions of *responsibility* and *craftsmanship*. In terms of responsibility, one may assume that a journalist takes responsibility for her work, accepting her privileged role in providing people with news as a product or service that they should be able to rely on to effectively act as citizens in democracy. Journalism is often understood in terms of actions and attitudes that set journalism apart from other professions. Understanding

journalism in terms of responsibilities, a common conceptualization of journalism is in terms of the specific set of ideological
commitments, such as the societal role journalists play, the
ethical standards of objectivity, trustworthiness and balance,
and independence, accuracy and currency as ideal-typical
standards (Deuze 2005).

Craftsmanship refers to a dedication "to do a job well for
its own sake" as Richard Sennett (2008: 9) describes it. In
this longterm and continuing process, the journalist involved
would develop and hone skills and rituals that enable her to
perfect the craft involved in carefully finding, verifying, and
reporting information of public interest. Such a definition
of journalism does not exclude more or less traditional
notions of the profession as carried out within the context of
venerable institutions such as the *New York Times*, the BBC,
O Globo, the *Asahi Shimbun* or *El País* – and neither does
it rule out what journalists are doing at any of the entities
documented in the online database Multiple Journalism
(multiplejournalism.org), or at any of the organizations
around the world that we document in this book. Indeed,
such a definition provides a useful alternative way of viewing
the field, which would allow us to consider the intention
behind work (responsibility and craftsmanship) rather than
the outcome and functions of the work.

Here we would like to pursue a more radical alternative,
however: rather than defining journalism, here we tell stories
by those who consider themselves journalists and/or are
defined as such by others. We focus on what their stories tell
us about how journalism may be many things at the same
time. We need, then, to highlight differences and find ways
to not simply explain them away in terms of a consistent
framework. Journalism is understood in many different ways,
and by foregrounding alternative conceptions we can open
up both the definition and the practice.

Journalism as dynamic and dispersed practice

We have to revisit the question of what journalism is for
conceptual considerations – the normative construction of

journalism through ideology and culture as reinforced in both scholarly work and professional publications – and practical propriety – given the increasingly fragmented, networked, and atypical nature of the labor market for newswork. When reconsidering this question, theory needs to move beyond the limitations framing this discussion: an overreliance on journalism as an inherently stable institution, distinct from other social systems. We must also go beyond its validation as uniquely necessary for democracy. These notions, however important, are beyond their sell-by date (Zelizer 2013). We argue for theorizing journalism from the ground up – focusing on where, how, by whom, and why "the lost labour of reporting" is done (Compton and Benedetti 2010: 487).

Until recently, the participation of journalists in the discursive construction of journalism was governed by being employed in (or, as a student, intern, or scholar, observing) a newsroom. The newsroom was the dominant form of employment and organization of work in journalism throughout the twentieth century. This arrangement served to stabilize the industry, going hand in hand with the shaping of consensual practices in journalism studies and education. The newsroom was the site to be a journalist, to be recognized as such, and scholars validated this process by pursuing empirical approaches dedicated to newsrooms and the newswork therein. Throughout the history of journalism studies high-profile and much-cited newsroom studies have appeared, from David Manning-White's (1950) work on the gatekeeping selections at a metropolitan newspaper, to seminal work by Jeremy Tunstall (1971) and Gaye Tuchman (1978), to more recent newsroom studies (see, for instance, Paterson and Domingo 2008; Domingo and Paterson 2011; Ryfe 2012; Usher 2014).

Even though these studies have been important in shedding light onto newsrooms, they focus on "problematic sites of fieldwork as well," as C. W. Anderson notes (2011: 152). Anderson points out that the traditional newsrooms "cannot serve as our only model for fieldwork" as "the very definition of journalism is being contested on a daily basis" (ibid.). This is not simply an operational problem in the current climate of newswork destabilization. The issue is more fundamental: throughout its history, scholars of journalism and the news have supported the dominance of certain interpretations of (the role of) journalism by focusing on specific institutional arrangements within particular privileged settings. As Karin Wahl-Jorgensen (2009: 23) puts it, the *newsroom-centricity* in journalism studies has meant that:

> scholars have tended to focus on journalists' culture as it emerges within the limited areas of newsrooms and other centralized sites for news production, usually paying scant attention to places, spaces, practices and people at the margins of this spatially delimited news production universe.

Such newsroom-centricity has implications beyond the mere privileging of some actors and exclusion of others: it has also led to an emphasis on "routinized and controlled forms and aspects of newswork" (ibid.: 25). The scholarly consensus on professional routines that make up newswork in newsrooms has been consolidated in journalism education, where such routines become fixed elements in the coursework for print, broadcast, and online sequences. Cottle notes how such a focus on "organizational functionalism" (2007: 10) privileges patterned ways of doing newswork over differentiation and divergence. What is more, within newsroom-centered research, scholars have privileged print over other media – and particularly over the dominant medium for news worldwide, television, further limiting the range of understanding and definition of journalism (Conway 2017). Moreover, the scholarly focus on elite, prestige, and glamorous institutions located in large cities of the capitalist Western world serves to solidify such places as the only ones deemed worthy of a voice to articulate what journalism is and who counts as a journalist (Nerone 2013). This fetishizing (Garnham 2000: 86) of legacy news media as the dominant institutions worthy of examination additionally finds its way into the curricular materials of journalism programs in the form of the kind of examples used, names referenced, and cases privileged over others – such as net-native journalism startups, community media, and independent news platforms (all of which are featured as cases in this book).

As much of newsgathering, editing, and packaging takes place elsewhere, outside of the newsroom, and with organizations virtualizing their workflow, delegating work to stringers and correspondents on the road, Wahl-Jorgensen (2009) notes how the newsroom is disappearing. Anderson (2011) advocates "blowing up the newsroom" when conducting contemporary newswork studies, proposing an approach that would consider news production as a network that transcends organizational boundaries. And yet, Anderson (2011: 160) concludes: "The newsroom is not extinct. In many ways, it is more important than ever, for it remains, even now, a central locus in which a variety of fragmented actor-networks find themselves tied together to create an occupation."

It is a challenge to consider journalism as a networked practice involving a distributed variety of actors and actants (Lewis and Zamith 2017), including an emerging global startup scene of newswork, while at the same time recognizing the permanence of meaning-giving structures such as the newsroom (Westlund and Lewis 2014; De Maeyer 2016). The more or less formal (and professional) arrangement of journalism requires an awareness of the *inhabited* nature (Hallett and Ventresca 2006) of the spaces where newswork takes place. The newsroom as an inhabited institution on the one hand provides the raw materials and guidelines for the way people work. On the other hand, the various people, technologies, and material infrastructures (including office furniture and architecture) moving in and out of the newsroom produce the institutions through their interactions. They put it into motion. The focus in this conceptualization of newswork is on *institutional complexity* (Delbridge and Edwards 2013: 927), and heterogeneous understandings of occupational membership (Bechky 2011: 1157). The point is not to say that contemporary news institutions are inhabited, and those in the past were not. As Carlson (2015: 2) suggests, journalism has always already been "a varied cultural practice embedded within a complicated social landscape. Journalism is not a solid, stable thing to point to, but a constantly shifting denotation applied differently depending on context."

The roles of institutions in newswork are dynamic and changing, opening our eyes to movement rather than stability, to how journalism is continuously *becoming* rather than what journalism *is*. This is to us the most profound challenge to journalism and journalism studies, something that starts with broadening and opening up definitions of what journalism is or could be: how to do justice to an object of study that is truly variegated? How to respect the way its participants engage in boundary work and solidifying practices as well as pursue the patterns of movement and transformation throughout?

Post-industrial journalism

As journalism continues to transform into a complex, networked, and fragmented profession that spills over into related media disciplines (such as marketing, advertising, and business communication) and across a wide variety of professional contexts (such as editorial collectives, startups, production studios, freelancer networks), it is possible to speak of journalism as a post-industrial profession (Anderson, Bell, and Shirky 2012). The post-industrialization of journalism can be seen as part of a trend benchmarked by the creative industries – of which journalism is a part – more generally: a gradual shift from centralized and hierarchical modes of industrial production to what Castells (2010) labeled a "network enterprise." The networked form of enterprise is also at work in journalism, as the International Federation of Journalists and the International Labour Organization originally noted in a 2006 survey among journalism unions and associations in 38 countries from all continents. The report signaled the rapid rise of so-called atypical work in the media, documenting that close to one-third of journalists worldwide work in anything but secure, permanent, or otherwise contracted conditions. Since then, freelance journalism, independent news entrepreneurship, and the casualization of labor have become even more paramount, particularly among younger reporters and newcomers in the field (as well as for more senior journalists affected by the layoffs and downsizing so common across the news industry; see Mosco 2009; Nel 2010; Sherwood and O'Donnell 2018).

Whatever label applies to the richly diverse and complex arrangements of contemporary "x journalism" – liquid, post-industrial, networked, to name a few – the overall trend in the profession can be seen as constituting (and resulting from) an organization of work where individual practices are part of a profoundly precarious context. Reorganizations, managerial reshuffling, buyouts, layoffs, disruption, and innovation are the norm rather than the exception. Working environments where the material context of newswork and the people journalists work with are in a state of constant flux, and careers in which someone's job trajectory looks more like the portfolio of an artist than the ascension ladder following an established professional hierarchy are part of this world. In response, practitioners develop new tactics, new self-conceptions, new values, and new organizational structures – while older structures, routines, and definitions (of news values) persist. Journalism in its post-industrial context is therefore best seen as a highly variegated phenomenon – a profession that is not limited to the institutions publishing and promoting the news that we have traditionally looked at when defining and understanding journalism. Our central argument in this book is that we need to theorize contemporary journalism as a complex and evolving ensemble of attitudes, activities, emotions, perceptions, and values of (organizations, groups or teams of) individuals: it is not a stable object, but continuously comes into being through each enactment of these elements. Such focus on the processual (as well as situational) nature of journalism is what allows us insight into the diversity and complexity of journalism.

By way of context, in this chapter, we highlight four major trends transpiring in journalism that signal a shift away from journalism as a stable and consensual field and toward a more dynamic notion of the profession. These four trends are: a concurrent reorganization of working environments; fragmentation of newswork; an emerging redactional society; and the ubiquity of media-making technologies. These trends point to a more networked (rather than an institutional) perspective of the journalist and a need to reconceptualize the field (Beckett 2008; van der Haak, Parks, and Castells 2012).

First, what Sennett (2006) calls the "culture of the new capitalism" draws our attention to the individualized nature of working and being at work. Whether contracted or independent, media workers are increasingly expected to embrace and embody an "enterprising" mindset, where every individual becomes a self-directed and self-disciplining brand or company. The journalist as an enterprising self reconstitutes "workers as more adaptable, flexible, and willing to move between activities and assignments and to take responsibility for their own actions and their successes and failures" (Storey, Salaman, and Platman 2005: 1036). Shifting the notion of enterprise – with its connotations of efficiency, productivity, empowerment, and autonomy – from the company to the individual uproots the traditional professional identity of newsworkers as structurally shielded from business concerns. Who you are as a journalist in a post-industrial context becomes as much about managing and promoting a business (whether that business is a news story or report, a news company or brand) as it is about your craft as a reporter and the responsibility you take for the work you have done to produce a truthful account of what happened.

Second, the production of news increasingly takes place both within and outside of professional news organizations, and within and across multiple media forms and formats. This fragmentation of newswork is facilitated by practices of outsourcing, subcontracting, and offshoring. The practice of such functional flexibility in the workforce is common throughout the news industry. Functional flexibility relates to the division of the workforce into a multiskilled core and a large periphery of semi-affiliated- professionals. The multiskilled core consists of a few professionals enjoying greater job security and career development who perform many different tasks throughout the organization. The peripheral group tends to be temporarily employed in subcontracted or projectized arrangements, and consists mainly of independent individual contractors working within a volatile and generally quite informally governed project ecology (Grabher 2002) of people both inside and outside traditional news institutions.

Third, on a more abstract level, in today's advanced communicational democracies, society can be conceptualized as redactional (Hartley 2000). A redactional society is one where editorial and transmedia work (Fast and Jansson 2019) are a required part of anyone's survival in the digital age, and therefore cannot be considered to be exclusive to a particular professional group such as journalists employed at news organizations. Traditionally, successful living in the information age was seen as dependent on being an *informational* as well as an *informed* citizen (Schudson 1995): next to being saturated in information, citizens needed to have "a point of view and preferences with which to make sense of it" (ibid.: 27). In redactional societies, simply having access to and making sense of information is not enough. What were originally deemed to be journalistic skills and competences are required for all citizens. In order to function effectively in contemporary society, people need to know how to gather and process vast amounts of information, weigh and sift the information at hand, and be able to do something purposefully with that information – using a great many information and communication technologies (Fast and Jansson 2019). In this digital era everyone, at some point, commits "acts of journalism" (Stearns 2013: 2), using what are deemed journalistic techniques and bearing the responsibility for the consequences of their communications.

The last trend that we want to mention as framing newswork in terms of the individual is the pervasive and ubiquitous role that (ever-developing) technologies play in the changing nature of journalistic work and organization. Today's printing press is the desktop or laptop personal computer equipped with broadband internet access and outfitted with easy-to-use publishing tools, open-source software applications, and converged hardware (camera, microphone, keyboard). These technologies have resulted in converged journalism within newsrooms; they have also facilitated the production of all aspects of journalism beyond newsrooms. This features centrally the multiskilled journalist who performs a greater variety of tasks – including those that were traditionally performed by others (whether designers, marketers, publishers, or editors).

Beyond journalism

In this fragmented, networked context of contemporary newswork we can signal a gradual increase in pressure on journalism as a profession (Witschge and Nygren 2009). A variety of factors drive this: shifting market demands and financial expectations; an atypical division of labor that fragments the profession; an ongoing erosion of its values and practices through the intervention of technology (including the advent of interfaces, algorithms, drones, and robotics to select, organize, report, publish, and distribute the news); a continuing state of flux engendered by bureaucratic and organizational upheaval; an altogether unstable and fluctuating trust in the public sector generally; a concomitant decline of trust in journalism specifically; and an increasing need for doing emotional work as part of newswork. Journalism, in this case, mirrors a deprofessionalization of classic professions in knowledge societies more generally, where the self-determination intrinsic to professionalism continues to erode:

> Professionals are forced to adapt to social changes, capitalist pressures, and consumerist tendencies that resist autonomous, closed-off occupational spheres. Professionals must *prove* their added value. In addition, professionals are forced to adapt to organizational and bureaucratic realities ... professionals have become part of large-scale organizational systems, with cost control; targets; indicators; quality models; and market mechanisms, prices, and competition. (Noordegraaf 2007: 763)

Noordegraaf considers these developments across many professions, finding that the response of knowledge workers tends to (re-)professionalize in hybrid ways by *reflexive control*. They search for personal, meaningful uses of professionalism, and seek to establish connections between clients, work, and organized networks (Rossiter 2006). This means journalists look for new ways of connecting to each other and to their professional ideals beyond the institutional contexts of newsrooms and trade unions by:

- forming editorial collectives;
- joining informal online associations (for example in moderated Facebook and LinkedIn groups);
- setting up shop together (generally in startup contexts, as is the primary focus of this book);
- participating in all kinds of online and offline network activities such as public debates, grassroots associations like the global Hacks/Hackers network (online at: hackshackers.com), workshops and conferences – most well-known the annual International Journalism Festival in Perugia, Italy (online at: journalismfestival.com).

Professionalism in a post-industrial context can therefore be seen as hybrid, where the vestiges of traditional occupational closure still exist next to (and blended with) more networked and reflexive ways of defining and maintaining a sense of professional autonomy.

For scholars in this field, it is of critical importance to go beyond capturing a snapshot of journalism at a particular time, freezing certain phenomena as if they are stable. It is crucial to focus on the diversity and processual nature of journalism: to show how the practices of journalism are constituted within their social context, to acknowledge the variety of actors involved in this process. It is important to trace the changing definitions of who is and who is not considered a journalist, as well as the precarious and shifting nature of newswork. The ultimate aim of our project is not to "pin down" journalism and its role in society, but rather to reflect on and make space for the multitude of ever-shifting practices and their varying impact in society. Such research has to rely not only on a variety of vantage points, but also on a variety of methods and theoretical perspectives to consider the becoming of journalism, so as to enable the telling of many stories about it. Moreover, to do justice to its complexity, such triangulation needs to allow for varying definitions to coexist, to allow various insights, even (or especially) when they contradict each other. It is in this space of doubt and insecurity that a deeper and more complex understanding of journalism in the digital age can come into being (Costera-Meijer 2016).

2
Setting the Scene: Startups

To broaden our understanding of what is defined as journalism and practiced under its label, it is particularly relevant to look at agents of media innovation (Westlund and Lewis 2014) and pioneering communities (Hepp 2016) in the field. Specifically, in this time of flux, witnessing firsthand how the shaping of journalism is taking place is fundamentally important to understanding changes in flows of information and in the societal roles of the profession. In order to operationalize the overall trend toward a post-industrial, dynamic, and highly diverse journalism around the world, we focus on a particular group of actors who are important in shaping what the profession is becoming: startup journalists. These journalists change the rules of the game by striking out on their own, charting new territory; they challenge the authority and position of legacy media, and in so doing become role models for others. By focusing on these actors, we aim to address those practices and processes of meaning-making that expand the scope, relevance, and understanding of journalism.

Through our studies of journalists and the startups they co-found we hope to add valuable stories of those in the field who are looking to broaden the concept of what journalism is. We are especially interested in those stories that move us toward a more inclusive, diverse understanding of journalism and its practices, roles, and functions in our communities and society at large. We focus in particular on startup journalists as important voices in the shaping of the changing practices and changing definitions of journalism (see also Hepp and Loosen 2018). Although their impact in terms of audience reach and name recognition may be limited when compared to legacy brands (such as the *New York Times* or the BBC), the ways they shape professional identity in the context of a highly uncertain, precarious, and challenging context remind us of what it takes to make things work as an independent media maker.

In the main, startup journalists see their mission as striving for technological as well as ideological innovation (see Wagemans, Witschge, and Harbers 2019), and to further the societal role attributed to journalism (Witschge and Harbers 2018a). They are generally deeply aware of the role they play in defining journalism and what it is for – in part, this is what motivates journalists to band together to form their own company or collective to begin with. What makes these actors of even greater interest – why we devote this book to their stories – is that they are not easily captured: they often do not fit neat boxes (definitions of journalism and what a "real" journalist is); the fleeting nature of their working arrangements makes them hard to find and sample; and their practices and discourses both confirm and challenge traditional concepts of the profession.

The cases discussed in this book all illustrate how the practice and concept of journalism is an ongoing, context-specific, and highly diverse process, profoundly shaped by the affective nature of newswork in general, and building a news operation from the ground up in particular. They challenge the way in which scholars have tended to theorize journalism as a static and fixed object, and show that the dichotomies that we have long held at the center of our analysis of journalism are not as informative as they seem to be. The professionals in our study (seemingly without problem) marry "neutrality" with "engagement," "subjectivity" with "objectivity," and "informing" with "activating" the audience. As Andrea Wagemans, Tamara Witschge, and Frank Harbers (2019) explain, the practitioners combine practices and definitions that we have previously labeled incompatible or contradictory in journalism studies. Our book serves to both document and celebrate the contradictions and diversity in journalism and of journalisms.

In this chapter we will provide the context of what we can call a "startup culture" in journalism. We highlight some of its main features and introduce the cases researched for this book, as well as the methods used for the research we and our students conducted.

Startup culture around the world

The picture conjured in our work – of increasingly networked, independent, precarious working conditions for journalists (and media workers more generally) – corresponds with trends in the labor market as a whole, showing a continuous growth of independent businesses and freelance entrepreneurship.[1] During this period – roughly since the start of the twenty-first century – news organizations have opted for major budget cuts, reorganizations, and considerable downsizing. Similar to the traditional intermediaries in other cultural industries (such as record labels in music, studios in film and television, holding firms in advertising), news publishers and broadcasters increasingly focus their investments on marketing and distribution, outsourcing production or acquiring content elsewhere.

The number of professionals permanently employed in content-creating positions in news organizations is dwindling rapidly. In the context of technological disruption, loss of traditional sources of revenue and changing audience preferences, production practices change. The people still working in the contemporary newsroom are often involved in more than the production of news. Managers and employers have come to stress the importance of "enterprise" as an individual rather than organizational or firm-based attribute (Du Gay 1996), in effect forcing entrepreneurialism on employees and freelancers alike (Oakley 2014). Although the notion of the enterprising or entrepreneurial individual extends beyond the media industries, the emergence of the enterprising professional in journalism is a relatively recent phenomenon. It coincides with a gradual breakdown of the wall between the commercial and editorial sides of the news organization, following a process of ongoing commodification of the media workplace, in which market pressures are increasingly dominating content decisions (von Rimscha 2015).

Faced with difficult and disruptive challenges on many fronts, the news business demands that its workers increasingly shoulder the responsibility of the company (or companies, in the case of those with patchwork careers, managing a portfolio of multiple clients). Trends such as the integration of the business and editorial sides of the news organization; the ongoing convergence of print, broadcasting, and online news divisions into digital-first and mobile-first journalism enterprises; and the introduction of projectized workstyles show that such hybridized working practices are not particular to freelance journalists. The difference between freelance and contracted workers is therefore a false dichotomy, as journalists working anywhere in the contemporary news industry experience insecurity and transformation quite alike.

Shifting the notion of enterprise from the level of the company to the individual suggests that it is a necessary part of the professional identity of each and every worker, contingently employed or not. Here we focus, however, on the trend of entrepreneurial journalism as it is located outside of legacy media. In the enterprising economy, entrepreneurial journalists increasingly start their own companies – somewhat similar to their colleagues elsewhere in the creative sector starting boutique advertising agencies or independent record labels, forming editorial or reportorial collectives as well as business startups. The emergence of a startup culture is indeed global: Since the early years of the twenty-first century, new independent (and generally small-scale and online-only) journalism companies have formed around the world.[2] The media discourse about entrepreneurial journalism tends to frame the trend and practice in a consistently positive way, generally suggesting that entrepreneurship is acceptable and uncontroversial, and even vital for survival in a digital age (Vos and Singer 2016).

This shift in focus to entrepreneurialism has not only taken place within the industry and in media discourse. Researchers and educators have matched this attention with scholarly work and curricular innovation, which further urges journalists to take on entrepreneurialism as a core element in their identity. Courses and degrees in entrepreneurial journalism are developed in countries around the world. Emphasizing individual traits, skills, attitude, and mindset, such curricular interventions tend to be premised on a future of journalism shaped by journalists who (alone or in collaboration) are able to monetize content in innovative ways, connect to publics in interactive new formats, grasp opportunities, and respond to (and shape) their environment (Briggs 2012).

There are a number of problematic issues with this idea of entrepreneurialism. First, even though we can find some optimism among the independently employed, studies consistently show adverse psychosocial effects, rising levels of stress, and overall poor subjective health among atypically employed media workers (Ertel et al. 2005; Hesmondhalgh and Baker 2011; Cohen 2015). The real or perceived freedom of working as an independent comes at a cost to many. In presenting the entrepreneur as a "savior" (Sørensen 2008), there is little attention for those costs. Even though the literature and case histories of entrepreneurship clearly suggest that most small-to-medium-sized businesses fail, there is very little attention paid to failure (but see Brouwers 2017) and the price thereof. In the overly optimistic discourse of entrepreneurialism, failure in fact tends to be seen as beneficial, and therefore unproblematic (Villi and Picard 2018).

A second conceptual issue regarding entrepreneurship in journalism is the fact that it is generally presented as an individual-level attribute, which tends to reinforce a "you are on your own" credo of individualized patchwork career trajectories. This perspective on entrepreneurship fits the approach taken by policymakers and scholars alike since the late 1990s, redefining media and cultural industries in terms of "creative industries," a term introduced by the British Department of Culture, Media and Sport in 1998, referring to those industries "which have their origin in individual creativity, skill and talent and which have a potential for wealth and job creation through the generation and exploitation of intellectual property."[3] The widespread adoption of this conflation of "industry" and the individual, and of "creativity" with commercial success can be seen as the specific context within which the debate about entrepreneurialism in media in general and journalism in particular takes place.

Entrepreneurship is thus presented as micro-level agency to make something happen (and be successful in the market), while the structural, unequal, and often arbitrary conditions underlying production processes do not get addressed. As Hans Landström and Bengt Johannisson remind us, "entrepreneurship [is] a phenomenon that lies beyond individual attributes and abilities. Entrepreneurship encompasses ... the organising of resources and collaborators in new patterns according to perceived opportunities" (2001: 228). It is imperative to understand entrepreneurial journalism in terms of both formal and informal networks, teams, and associations that tend to transcend the boundaries of news organizations large and small, and that can have idealistic, cultural, as well as commercial goals and aspirations. In other words: we need to engage entrepreneurship in journalism not just as a new or innovative way to make money in an otherwise risky *economic* context, but also as a *social* challenge or opportunity to be a journalist in precarious times.

In this context we find that the contemporary news organization, both large and small, is not so much a *place* but a *process*, which involves shifting networks of people, technologies, and spaces. There is a high degree of flux, blurring the in/out boundary of the newsroom and its environment, as well as the "church and state" separation between the editorial and business side of things. In fact, the new ways in which newswork is organized ask us to move beyond binary oppositions, primarily the one of inside and outside the newsroom as the supposed "heart" of autonomous newswork. As this notion becomes ever more obsolete, the concept may obfuscate rather than illuminate what it is like to be a journalist. It is important to emphasize that most of the actual reportorial work gets done elsewhere, and that journalistic acts coincide with a whole range of other, related, and synergistic activities necessary to "make it work." With the rise of post-industrial journalism, the journalistic workforce becomes distributed, consisting of (a declining group of) contracted employees, individual entrepreneurial journalists, freelance editorial collectives, and a worldwide emergence of news startups.

The emergence of a startup culture in the field of journalism is global: since the early years of the twenty-first century, new independent (and generally small-scale and online-only) journalism companies have formed around the world (Bruno and Kleis Nielsen 2012; Simons 2013; Coates Nee 2014; Küng 2015; Powers and Zambrano 2016). The context consists of self-deleterious print and broadcast business models, audiences migrating to the digital space where their time is spent less with visiting news websites but more with finding and sharing news via social media (thereby enabling companies like Facebook and Google to further siphon off advertising revenue), and an organizational context rife with atypical working conditions, ongoing managerial overhauls, and declining budgets. Faced with these conditions, journalistic newcomers and senior reporters alike strike out on their own.

Case studies

Our book documents a five-year project charting the development of news startups around the world, seeking to understand the ways digital journalism takes shape in the context of new organizational forms and new operational practices. In our project we critically investigate the work of those who are called "entrepreneurial" or "startup" journalists in a variety of settings and countries. The ongoing project at the time of going to print covers 22 cases in 11 countries (see Table 1), and was partly funded through a nonresidential fellowship with the Donald W. Reynolds Journalism Institute at the Missouri School of Journalism in the United States.[4] In total over 125 people were interviewed by a research team consisting of 24 graduate students and us (see also the Prologue to this book).

Our identification of startups in the field follows that of Bruno and Nielsen (2012) and Powers and Zambrano (2016): organizations built primarily around a web presence, that have no formal affiliation with legacy news media, and that seek recognition by their peers as journalistic. That said, over the years some companies have ended up participating in our project because of opportunity sampling, not fitting neatly into this original operationalization. At the time of writing this book, some of our students opted to focus on the growing trend of intrapreneurial initiatives within legacy institutions seeking to replicate the startup model (these cases are not included in the dataset used for this book). In general, the aim has not been to get to a representative sample, but rather to assemble a selection of cases that gives us an appropriate amount of variety, range, and depth, thus allowing us to tell many different stories of what is happening under the label of journalism.

Table 1: Startups in the Beyond Journalism project (phase: 2014–18)[5]

Name Startup	Country	Remarks	Start	Year of research
360 Magazine	Netherlands	Largely subscription-based print magazine with Dutch translations of international journalism; partnership with Courrier International (France). https://www.360magazine.nl/	2011	2015
Alaska Dispatch	United States	Online-only news site combined with print newspaper (since 2014). Declared bankruptcy in 2017	2008	2016
Bureau Boven	Netherlands	Freelance female-only editorial collective; numerous jointly funded projects (also non-journalistic). http://www.bureauboven.com/	2013	2015
Code4SA	South Africa	Nonprofit data journalism outfit (part of international network Code4); sponsoring and civil society contracts. Became Openup in 2017: https://openup.org.za/	2013	2014
Common Reader	United States	University-based journal with in-depth news articles and opinion pieces. https://commonreader.wustl.edu/	2014	2016
Corner Media Group	United States	Network of hyperlocal online news sites in New York City; advertising-based. https://bklyner.com/	2011	2016
De Corre-spondent	Netherlands	Online magazine; long-form articles; access is membership-based, also foundation support. https://decorrespondent.nl/	2013	2014
Discourse Media	Canada	Collaboration of freelance investigative journalists; story packages; foundation support and news organizations. https://www.thediscourse.ca/	2013	2017

Follow The Money	Netherlands	Membership-based startup for financial-economic investigative journalism. https://www.ftm.nl/	2010	2014
InkaBinka	United States	Software developer for automated news summaries; subscription-model and venture capital. Ceased publication in 2017	2013	2015
IRPI	Italy	Investigative journalism platform; nonprofit with (international) foundation support, crowdfunding. https://irpi.eu/en/	2012	2014
Jaaar	Iran	Jaaar is an online kiosk for newspaper articles (similar to Blendle in The Netherlands). https://www.jaaar.com/	2011	2015
La Silla Vacía	Colombia	Independent news blog; crowdfunding and (US) foundation support. https://lasillavacia.com/	2009	2014
Mediapart	France	Subscription-based online in-depth news platform; also user-generated content. https://www.mediapart.fr/	2007	2014
Media-storm	United States	Film production and interactive design studio, with clients in journalism, business, and education. https://mediastorm.com/	2005	2016
MMU Radio	Uganda	University-based community radio station; international funding. https://www.facebook.com/MountainsoftheMoonUniversity/	2016	2015
Naya Pusta	Nepal	Weekly children's TV news show; international foundation support; produced by the Nepal Forum of Environmental Journalists. http://www.nayapusta.com/	2012	2015
The Brooklyn Ink	United States	University-based (and sponsored) local investigative student news website; offered as a course. Last post in December 2017	2007	2016
The Post Online	Netherlands	Free online news blog; some investment backing. Partnership with TPO Magazine. https://tpo.nl/	2009	2014
TPO Magazine	Netherlands	Online news magazine; people subscribe to individual journalists, also crowdfunding; partnership with The Post Online. Became ReportersOnline in 2015: https://reportersonline.nl/	2013	2014
Zetland	Denmark	Online magazine co-created with members; also: live journalism shows in theaters. https://www.zetland.dk/	2012	2018

In all these cases, we explore and interrogate the factors involved in creating and running a journalism startup, and how the professionals involved give meaning to what they do in the fast-changing field of digital journalism. We aim to shed light on the ways in which these new startups influence the field and inflect the wider understanding of journalism, providing rich, in-depth descriptions of these new forms of journalism, the new ways of making it work, and new ways of practicing and perceiving journalism.

This project defines journalism as an open practice in which a variety of actors and many activities are involved. It moves away from more conventional institutional, newsroom, and genre-based understandings of journalism (see also Witschge and Harbers 2018b). Due to the limited time in which we had access to the various startups, our analysis of everyday activities was generally limited to observing a handful of meetings and spending a few days to up to a few weeks in the various workspaces. For the analyses in this book we focused in the main on the discursive nature of journalism: how practitioners talk about their work, perceptions, emotions, values, and their role in society – to name a few areas we addressed in interviews and more informal conversations. We thus aimed to lay bare the various meanings the participants gave to their work and practices (Couldry 2004), and sought to situate these stories within our observations and our analyses of the output of the startups, as well as in relation to a comparative assessment of all the other cases we looked at.

With each case, we have followed a baseline method. First, we established contact with the key people involved. Our experience has been that getting access is relatively easy if one is prepared to go beyond typical high-profile news startups (such as Vox, Politico, and Quartz in the United States). The next step was to set up the parameters of access, as we tried to get the organization involved to allow for site visits and observation of workplace practices (such as editorial meetings, tagging along with reportorial projects, hanging out in dedicated office environments wherever these may be) over the course of several weeks.

Second, during the site visits – and in some cases, before or afterwards via phone or Skype – the visiting researcher would conduct as many interviews as possible with the startup founders, employees (if any), professionals involved, as well as some context interviews with other journalists working in the same area. For comparative purposes an interview guide was developed (after a few pilot studies in our home country, The Netherlands), consisting of semi-structured questions on:

- People's professional backgrounds;
- Practices, competences and skills involved in running the startup and doing the work;
- The organization and management of labor as well as the production process;
- The material context of the startup (i.e., workspaces, hardware and software, technologies involved);
- Professional identity – focusing on ethics, role perceptions, status and reputation, news values, motivations and goals, perspectives on audience, community and society; and the affective dimension of work;
- And, to wrap up, a final question on what the journalists involved considered as the most fundamental challenge for the field of (professional) journalism.

A third empirical step consisted of securing access to internal and external documentation on the startup. Internal documents include meeting notes, e-mail exchanges, and (draft) papers related to the journalistic, managerial, and business practices of the organization. External documents include press statements and public mission statements (including online "About" and "FAQ" sections), social media posts (blog posts, tweets, Facebook status updates, contributions to Instagram/Pinterest/LinkedIn, and so on), interviews given to other media, and press clippings on the startup involved.

A fourth step involved doing a comprehensive survey of the products and services the startup produced during the time of our investigation. In some cases, this involved doing a content analysis of stories; in other cases this phase of the research covered a detailed description of all the features of the output the startup had been able to generate.

Last, the data were coded by one of the researchers on the team, Andrea Wagemans, using TAMS Analyzer (a native open-source Macintosh qualitative research tool), with a combination of pre-established coding categories and interpretative open coding, deriving further categories from the data. This resulted in a final list of 118 categories that were used to analyze the data for the chapters of this book.

We have complemented these data with insights gained from the literature, from responses by practitioners in the field, and remarks that researchers expressed in informal conversations or formal settings (public lectures, conferences, meetings). Also, insights from two other projects have been integrated where relevant: the New Beats and the Entrepreneurship at Work projects. New Beats[6] is an internationally comparative study supported by a Discovery grant from the Australian Research Council (ARC Project ID DP150102675) administered by Lawrie Zion and Tim Marjoribanks at LaTrobe University, to which project Mark is attached as a Principal Investigator. The focus of the study is on how newsworkers experience the end of their careers – either through being laid off or taking early retirement. It explores the role of mass redundancies, forced career changes, and the digital reinvention of professional journalism at a time of industry restructuring and technological change.

The research consisted of an online survey among working journalists who (since 2012) had been forced out of their contract or who decided to resign. Between 2012 and 2016 well over a thousand journalists were made redundant in The Netherlands (out of a total population of approximately 18,000 working journalists).[7] In the Dutch version of the project we additionally conducted a series of in-depth video interviews with prominent journalists to reflect on their careers and the development of journalism as a profession. Earlier surveys were conducted by colleagues in Australia (Sherwood and O'Donnell 2018; Zion et al. 2016; O'Donnell, Zion, and Sherwood 2016) and the United Kingdom (Nel 2010). The Dutch project was carried out in collaboration with the national association of journalists (Nederlandse Vereniging voor Journalisten, NVJ) and the Netherlands Institute for Sound and Vision. This project accounts for the complex interplay between economic, technological, workplace, and career pressures reshaping professional journalism, as experienced by journalists. The survey ran during September 2016. Respondents were chosen through self-selection after the NVJ distributed a call to participate among its members.

In total 77 (former) journalists responded to the request. Between the fall of 2016 and spring of 2017, a total of seven additional oral history video interviews were conducted.[8]

The project "Entrepreneurship at Work: Analysing Practice, Labour, and Creativity in Journalism" (funded by the Dutch national science organization NWO, dossier 276-45-003) is run by Tamara and aims at theorizing emerging shared understandings, everyday work activities, and material contexts of entrepreneurial journalists to understand how these challenge traditional conceptualizations of journalism. To do so, it adopts a practice-theory approach (Witschge and Harbers 2018b), and employs a multi-methodological framework to capture the practices in the various stages of the journalistic process. It combines interviewing with enactment research, where two PhD students (Amanda Brouwers and Sofie Willemsen) have set up their own startup, using auto-ethnography to research their experiences in the process. Here, we draw on insights from interviews with startups where relevant.

Before we tell the stories of the startup journalists throughout the world, we would like to highlight two general observations to provide some context to what we see as relevant for startup culture: how the personal motivations of the professionals involved really matter to our understanding of what (entrepreneurial) journalism is, and how these newsworkers reflect on their own careers, ambitions, and aspirations in the context of opting to work outside of the legacy news media system. We would like to share these overall observations we made during this five-year period of talking with newsworkers, supervising graduate students, visiting startups, and presenting our work-in-progress at academic, professional, as well as public conferences – as we deem them relevant for countering major ways of speaking about entrepreneurial journalism. Rather than simply telling stories about startup success or sustainability – particularly in economic terms – in this book we focus on the ways in which these journalists relate to and thus contribute to shaping journalism through their perspectives, perceptions, discourses, output, activities, behavior, and emotions as expressed and reflected upon in interviews, observations, and interactions. Our aim is to provide rich and diverse stories about the ways in which journalism is practiced and defined.

To do so, we have organized the book around themes that came up prominently in the data. These themes signpost the ways in which the journalists relate to their work internally (what drives them personally), externally (how they work), and societally (the public impact they aspire to with their work). To let the stories speak more directly, we insert boxes highlighting particular themes by providing in-depth insight into one of the specific startups researched.

The two themes featured prominently at all the startups in our sample, regardless of national, cultural, economic, or technological contexts, were: the structure of their motivations and goals in pursuing their dream of journalism by going at it alone (that is: deliberately operating outside the legacy media system); and their reflections on the potentially precarious features of the global startup trend for the future of journalism and the consequences for their own career choices. These themes, albeit articulated differently at the various sites we visited in this project, came up time and time again and benefit from exploration before we dive into specific accounts. By discussing the way in which a variety of motivations and goals play parts in the way these pioneer communities make sense of their work, we aim to show that there is not one neat conceptualization of the aims of those working in the industry. The variety of goals and motivations at play highlight the fact that economic goals are only one motivation among many. Second, by addressing the precarious features of startup culture we wish to stress that we do not uncritically embrace entrepreneurship as the answer to the many challenges that journalism faces. Yes, we focus on startup journalists and address how they practice and conceptualize journalism in new ways, acting like pioneers. Their enthusiasm and energy is infectious and inspiring. At the same time there are most certainly costs, challenges, and critical issues that arise with startup culture.

Motivations and goals

The post-industrialization of journalism is part of a longterm trend. Freelance journalism, independent entrepreneurship, and flexibilization of working conditions have become paramount throughout the profession, particularly among younger reporters and newcomers in the field (as well as for more senior journalists affected by the layoffs and downsizing so common across the news industry). One would expect that the dominant reason for setting up shop on one's own would be the crisis in journalism in terms of employment. Whenever a crisis in journalism was mentioned, however, our participants would refer to it in terms of a business opportunity: to fill a news gap. Examples of mentioned markets are taking children seriously as a news audience (Nepal), identifying information and communication technologies as a valuable niche news segment (Iran), or offering in-depth stories with a more engaged or "subjective" voice than would be common among legacy news titles (France, Italy, Denmark, The Netherlands, the United States). In fact, the most commonly mentioned motivations for starting a business among the cases we investigated – bearing in mind the challenge of generalizing from case studies – fall into four thematic categories, none of which related to the purported crisis in journalism: technological, economic, cultural, and social.

Regarding *technology*, startup founders would mention the advantages online publishing offers them in terms of cost efficiency. More specifically, though, their technological motivation tends to be exemplified by a sincere belief in the digital as a superior platform with which to gather, produce, co-create, and disseminate news. All phases of the journalistic production process run through an almost exclusively digital design, where information, leads, and sources are collected online (often via social media); stories and reports are written, edited, and produced in multimedia formats (combining various media, such as text, pictures, infographics, and video); audiences can be involved in various ways (from leaving comments on the site and encouraging further sharing online to user-generated content such as blog posts, up to and including crowdfunding as a business model); and distributing news and information online (in real time, through day-parting, or other creative temporal strategies), which offers freedom from print and broadcast schedules. Whereas in the old days technological complexity tended to push news organizations toward assembly-line production schedules that limited the range of possibilities for storytelling, the current digital context offers plenty of affordable opportunities via open source or pirated software. Online is not just a platform or a mode of publication – in the eyes of these pioneers working, publishing, and interacting, online offers a way to do "real" journalism, the kind of journalism they *want* to do, rather than the one they *have* to do. We find such idealization of technology as instrumental to the kind of journalism produced remarkable, perhaps similar to the love other journalists express for "the newspaper" as their medium of choice (referring to the smell and feel of the pages, and its privileged role in private and public life).

An *economic* motivation for investing time and resources into a startup relates to the pragmatic notion that working together provides the journalists involved a better chance at surviving than going it alone. Also, their capital – as in the ability to convert their resources, networks, contacts, reputation, skills, and competences into opportunities for business, funding, or access to sources of support – tends to be enhanced when banding together (see also Powers and Zambrano 2016). In numerous cases younger journalists or newcomers to the profession would work under the guidance or leadership of one or more senior reporters and editors.

A note of concern here refers to the efforts that journalists involved are making to make ends meet, even when banding together. Commonly, the key source of income for a startup – or for individual reporters associated with the startup – is non-journalistic: working for commercial clients, or within the parameters set by funding institutions. Additionally, much of the work that goes into designing, setting up, and maintaining a startup is in fact free labor – a form of work Karin Fast, Henrik Örnebring, and Michael Karlsson (2016: 969) call "prospective" labor, involving a kind of professional who "takes high risks, puts in long hours without any guaranteed reward, is likely to be exploited, but can also find nuggets so big they will never have to perform labour again." The latter motivation was absent in financial terms from the sample – with one exception: California-based InkaBinka's founders were aiming for a multimillion-dollar paycheck for their software development. The "nuggets" for our other interviewees consisted mainly of chances to tell stories that they personally felt really matter, have impact, and make a difference.

Another economic argument voiced referred to the freedom the more or less independent environment offered to pursue whatever our participants considered to be quality work, rather than being evaluated on the basis of criteria related to productivity. Legacy media counterparts were often dismissed for focusing too much on quantity over quality and caring more about producing to quota. We cannot test the veracity of such statements other than acknowledging that these claims serve a particular purpose: to validate the choice for going it alone, for choosing the precarious path of starting or joining a new small business with no job security, more often than not in nonpaid or underpaid circumstances.

As is shown in study after study, journalists around the world rate autonomy as most important when it comes to job satisfaction and happiness (Windahl and Rosengren 1978; Scholl and Weischenberg 1999; Willnat, Weaver, and Choi 2013). In their comparison of surveys among journalists from 31 countries, Lars Willnat, David Weaver, and Jihyang Choi (2013: 172) note:

> Patterns indicate that most journalists around the world recognize the importance of job autonomy, but also perceive large gaps between the ideal of autonomy and the actual freedoms they have. However, these gaps in perception are not restricted to nations with limited press freedom.

Regardless of whether the cases in our sample were from supposedly politically "free" countries such as the United States and The Netherlands or from nations with more restricted press policies such as Iran, a key *cultural* motivation for the journalists involved was to do what they felt like doing – to be free from what many perceived as the shackles and constraints of legacy media organizations. At the same time, such real or perceived autonomy comes at a cost, because it "is sufficiently powerful to override any misgivings, constraints or disadvantages that might emerge in the everyday repro-duction of this highly competitive and uncertain domain" (Banks 2007: 55). Objectively speaking, the working condi-tions at many of the startups in our sample were anything but good: people work all hours of the day and night, the boundary between working life and private life disappears, the work tends to be unpaid or underpaid, and there is little or no predictability about what may happen next to the work or company involved. Yet the relative freedom one has gets touted and celebrated throughout (for further critical consideration of this, see Brouwers and Witschge 2019).

Finally, a *social* motivation emerges from these case studies of journalism startups. Banding together, setting up shop with a group, working on projects as a team – these all offer solutions to social isolation as a side effect of working as an independent journalist in the field. The camaraderie and warm collegiality often found among the colleagues of these startups was palpable, often seducing us as researchers in the process. It becomes harder to remain neutral and observant when the people you are witnessing, interviewing, and studying are clearly passionate, and when they mutually validate each other's passions for the work, the company, the product, and the profession of journalism. At the same time, we have to note the distinct character of this collegiality as a rather loose network. Startups are fluid spaces in that they are inhabited by a temporary constellation of people, many of whom are either by necessity or accident also working on other things, scouting for other opportunities, and considering alternatives. It is a precarious collegiality, then, yet a highly appealing one.

The personal investment of journalists in their work is nothing new, of course. Classic studies on newsworkers – such as, most prominently, "The News Factory" published in 1980 by Charles Bantz, Suzanne McCorkle, and Roberta Baade, documenting the routinized workflow at a local television newsroom in the United States – seem to have predicted the motivations for journalists to leave established news organizations in favor of trying out journalism on their own terms. In this study, the consequences of news organizations that opted for a routinization of the production process were considered:

> The development of a factory news model, with its assembly line approach, in conjunction with the trends toward routinization appear to have at least four organizational consequences: (1)

the news factory lacks flexibility, (2) there is a lack of personal investment in the news product, (3) newswork becomes evaluated in productivity terms, and (4) goal incongruence emerges between newsworkers' job expectations and job reality. (Bantz, McCorkle, and Baade 1980: 59)

Seen in this light, the emergence of a startup culture at least in part stems from a significant frustration among (certain) journalists about (specific) legacy media business and managerial practices (Prenger and Deuze 2017).

Startups: Precarious features

Having addressed the motivations and goals of startup journalists, we wish to provide an additional, more critical note and address some problematic issues related to the precarious features of journalism in the context of new news organizations. First, in the context of this kind of journalism, we need to consider what can make up a coherent professional career. For some time now careers in media industries in general and journalism in particular have changed structure, from a more or less predictable linear progression (going from being an intern to a junior staffer, securing a contract to be reporter or correspondent, then moving up the ladder in the newsroom, at some point being eligible for an editorial position) to a portfolio career. Such a career includes a patchwork of assignments, contracts, projects, stories, media, positions, and duties – often in a rather random order, including numerous jobs not neces-sarily journalistic in nature. Still, such "portfolio worklives" (Handy 1989) tend to be seen and experienced as a series of stepping stones, leading to what – in hindsight – looks like a fairly consistent career trajectory. Despite the enthusiasm we found among many study participants (about their company and their work), what remains is the question of to what extent life (partly) inside a startup is sustainable and allows for personal and professional growth, given the fact that it is often cross-subsidized by other (non-journalistic) work, that it offers little control over what may happen next, and that it does not necessarily contribute to a specific reputation or status (which then can be marketed to secure future employment). This is the ultimate embodiment of precarity in work, as it is quite difficult for the professionals involved to have control over what happens next in their work lives. Pierre Bourdieu (1998) fiercely critiqued such precariousness of work in the digital age, suggesting that living under precarious conditions prevents rational anticipation and, in particular, the basic belief and hope in the future that one needs in order to (individually or collectively) rebel against intolerable working or living conditions.

A second, related concern with precariousness concerns work as an opportunity for (personal) growth. In the context of ever-increasing casualization of work throughout the contemporary labor market, where do workers learn new skills, how do they reflect in a structural way on their own process, and to what extent are there ample moments for mentoring, intervision, and learning? Professionalization tends to be tied up with a certain dedication to the craft – in this case, the craft of journalism. And indeed, the people in this study generally speak lovingly of journalism – what it can be, what it should be, what kind of impact it should have on society. There seems to be a clear commitment to quality and taking responsibility for the consequences of doing journalism, but how does one develop structures of learning and growth in such a precarious context? There seems to be a new role for unions and professional associations here – one that is less about protecting people's careers, and more about assisting in people's decisions (for example through education and training, legal assistance, and administrative support) regardless of what their chosen form of employment looks like.

A third element of concern is the current structure of the market for journalistic storytelling. The emerging networked nature of work and the emergence of a global culture of entrepreneurialism in journalism ideally bring about a situation where audiences can pick and choose from a tremendous amount of quality offerings available on a wide variety of platforms and channels. On the other hand, quite a few startups we studied rely in part on traditional (print and online) publishers or broadcasters to pay for and distribute their work. At the same time, these legacy media in recent years have laid off large numbers of journalists, effectively relying increasingly on freelancers and people working in otherwise contingent contractual contexts. This produces a market where journalists compete with each other for a chance to tell (and sell) stories, rather than the other way around: where publishers (online, print, radio, television, mobile) would contend for the best reporting and reporters around. Interestingly, in several places around the world new collective enterprises have sprung up in recent years aiming to organize freelance and independent journalists outside of traditional trade unions in an attempt to improve working conditions (including client negotiation support, healthcare provision, and workspace facilitation) for freelancers as a group. This kind of hybrid professionalism provides one possible solution to the dilemma of a distributed workforce that has little negotiating power vis-à-vis large companies or corporations. At the same time, many of the startups we studied opted out of this competition for recognition and access to legacy publication channels, instead building their own platform – varying from a radio station to theater performances, from websites and weblogs to printed magazines.

Finally, a word regarding the audience for journalism. In most of these startups significant efforts are made to engage the audience directly, by taking them seriously as a market or a constituency, at times asking them for input and expertise (both financially through crowdfunding and content-wise via crowdsourcing), and including them in the production process with user-generated and user-submitted content. This raises the question: how does one cultivate a genuine relationship with a public as an (entrepreneurial) journalist? One would expect that legacy media had an enormous head start toward this end, but we know from journalism studies that in fact most news media struggle significantly with their audience relationships, generally outsourcing the responsibility for it to marketing departments, ombudsmen, or audience representatives, sometimes including blogging or vlogging editors-in-chief. The dedication to the public that characterizes many of the startups in this study has been a remarkable (and laudable) feature. Yet many of these startups probably will not last, given the rate of failure for startups generally (Naldi and Picard 2012). A generally high turnover rate of journalists and editors in such small to medium-sized enterprises amplifies the volatility of the startup scene, and carefully cultivated relationships with a specific community may vanish overnight. Given the already rocky relationship between professional journalism and the general public, this could be a source of concern.

The bottom line is that journalism is a highly dynamic, exciting, precarious, fragmented, networked, diversified, and at times perilous profession in the process of constantly being constituted through the variety of activities of and discourses on journalism. Theoretically speaking this has always been the case – even if we, as scholars and journalism educators, have not always defined or operationalized the profession that way. Empirically and realistically, though, journalism today is moving beyond itself – and we hope that this project and book offer a glimpse of one possible trajectory in this trend.

3
Stories from the Heart

We deliberately start telling the stories of our startup journalists with a focus on the heart. Emotion plays a profound role in any consideration of (the future of) journalism: the often passionate and always affective commitment of journalists to what they do, their work and craft (Beckett and Deuze 2016; Siapera 2019). To be a professional, working journalist in the twenty-first century means, to most, having to go above and beyond the call of duty. Many (if not most) journalists today are engaged well beyond what any profession could ask for. In the networked news environment, journalists have to be deeply committed and involved well beyond the boundaries of (for example) a 9-to-5 existence, as their work is insecure, their pay limited, people's trust precarious, and their working time stretches beyond a predictable print deadline or broadcast schedule. More often than not the commitment of journalists to the work necessarily includes a fair amount of personal branding along with constant reskilling and multiskilling demanded by the rapidly and continuously changing technological context of media work. With the institutional protections and privileges of the profession limited, this means that the journalists' drive becomes increasingly personal.

The personal, affective, and emotional engagement with newswork needs to be considered carefully – even if it is largely absent from the literature. In an exception, Eugenia

Siapera and Ionna Iliadi discuss how "social activities, once thought private leisure activities, have now become a central, necessary and integral component of modern jobs, including journalism" (2015: 76). Journalism as a profession derives and extracts value from human relationships – from the camaraderie and club membership of the peer community of fellow reporters and editors to a medium's increasingly interactive (and sometimes co-creative) relationship with its community: from an independent journalist's attempt to manage and maintain her followers on social media to the incessant networking, pitching, and people-pleasing work that practitioners have to engage in to stay current and visible with an otherwise fragmented market for competitor-colleagues and clients.

What Siapera and Iliadi (2015) highlight, and what we stress here as a major point of consideration when researching media work in general and journalism in particular, is that journalism is affective labor to its practitioners. This takes the most private of emotions – including joy and laughter, but also frustration and anger – into the very public sphere of work. Once on the job, these emotions must be managed to achieve professional goals, such as building and sustaining communities around the news product or service, engaging in professional networking and reputation management, and overall maintaining good relationships with (potential) co-workers, clients, competitor-colleagues, and collaborators. Furthermore, one expects journalists to be able to handle their emotions when covering intense emotional events – from terrorist attacks to natural disasters, from neighborhood disputes to traffic accidents, from crimes to wars, including celebrity and politicians' scandals, meltdowns, and breakdowns. All of these and many more instances of newsworthy stories require significant emotional work to be performed by journalists and in various ways affect their emotional well-being (Zelizer and Allan 2011; Kotišová 2019) – on top of which they are also expected to tactically use emotions in their storytelling to increase audience attention and appeal (Pantti 2010), supposedly crafting an "experience of involvement" with the news (Peters 2011). In today's era of public engagement as a goal for journalism, it is crucial to note that promoting and participating in what

Seth Lewis (2014) calls "reciprocal journalism" comes at an emotional cost.

In their interviews (with mainly freelance journalists), Siapera and Iliadi find that affective labor requires "the investment of one's 'authentic' self, the investment of personal time, and the investment of care" (2015: 86). When engaging online, when participating in interactions with audiences, and when reporting on the community, journalists find that their credibility is benchmarked by who they are as "real" human beings, and their productivity in part consists of (stronger) social bonds with peers, competitor-colleagues, stakeholders, members of the community, and the audience at large. To be a journalist on the job, Siapera and Iliadi conclude, is not just a professional identity, but rather contingent on people bringing their "whole selves" to work.

It is exactly this aspect of work that we seek to highlight in this chapter. What does the everyday *workstyle* (how lifestyle and work are subsumed in the way of working and being at work; see Deuze 2007) look like for the professionals involved with news startups around the world? What is the emotional investment in (and emotional return from) the work they do?

The involvement of the heart first and foremost turns the work into a passion project: something to be done because of a higher calling, because they experience an intrinsic "need" to do this. The various participants would talk to us about giving up on other parts of their lives in order to make it work. Even more, they at times would give up on getting (or demanding) adequate pay for what they do. The calling of (startup, independent, and pioneering) journalism tends to be validated by the argument that it has become impossible to do this kind of work within the structures and limitations of legacy media organizations. What keeps the emotional involvement of these workers at peak levels is the feeling of truly contributing to a greater good – and sometimes that greater good can indeed be a personal good: achieving something for themselves, reaching a personal goal with their work.

We end this chapter by linking these stories from the heart with a specific notion of creativity and of being able to do something creative with journalism that runs throughout these cases: experimentation and innovation, without having to negotiate an already established news culture that would respond to such work with the fear of losing the credibility gained through history and tradition. We want to reiterate that we document these arguments and statements without celebration or critique. In short, although it is important to signal the profound cost of the journalists' emotional involvement without much power or agency to change the precarious circumstances of newswork, it is just as crucial to highlight the commitment so many (often quite young) practitioners still have to the professional ideals of providing a public service, taking responsibility for (and) telling the truth.

It would be easy to contrast the often romantic and idealistic stance of our interviewees with a "rational" or "realistic" voice of critique. Such suspicious reading (Felski 2015) can have much value, and we have engaged in it too. But in this project, we aim to provide the stories from the journalists as they experience and feel them – contradictions, unmet needs, and conflicting interests included. We feel that to understand these stories and their impact on journalism, a suspicious reading featuring a "spirit of skeptical questioning or outright condemnation, an emphasis on its precarious position vis-à-vis overbearing and oppressive social forces," and an "assumption that whatever is *not* critical must therefore be *un*critical" (Felski 2015: 2) is not what allows us to break open the field of (possible) journalisms. Indeed, we much prefer to keep speaking with the voice of our interviewees, who are much better at marrying diverse and paradoxical practices and definitions without simplistic reduction into binary distinctions (see also Witschge et al. 2019).

Passion for the profession

Journalists genuinely care about journalism. Despite misgivings about established media companies, about the management of the industry as a whole, or regarding the way people have come to distrust or avoid the news – practitioners still embrace the profession for its promise of enabling an open democratic society characterized by free speech and the free flow of information. Journalists self-identify strongly with the profession, referring to journalism as their "calling," "duty," or "moral obligation." Their comments suggest an intrinsic motivation (Witschge 2013) and emotional investment regarding the profession, much like a craftsman has an inherent desire to do her job well (Sennett 2008). This passion for journalism begets three distinct meanings in the discourse of those we interviewed: aesthetics, engagement, and emotional environment.

Making something beautiful, contributing to the growth and possible maturation of a new product or service, developing a business from the ground up and turning it into something that gets recognition from the outside world – the participating reporters and editors often alluded to these emotional drivers for their work. And as this particular quote illustrates, they put up with the downsides of the work in order to serve the higher end they identify with:

> What I would love to do exclusively is to make beautiful newspapers, magazines… . But yes, that is part of the reason I also do some copy writing on the side, because I have to. Well, you just have to produce work to make ends meet. Or you have to fully commit, like working seventy hours or more a week.

Aesthetic passion – the desire to make or contribute to something beautiful, something that has an impact, that stimulates people in one way or another to react – played a typical role in the conversations we and the researchers on the team had during the years of this project. Although it rarely gets acknowledged in the literature on journalism, it became clear that aesthetics (in terms of the desire to do something well when given the chance) plays a crucial role in journalists' passion for the profession.

A second element of journalism as a *passion project* relates to people's profound engagement with doing the work – to the exclusion of anything else, as this interviewee explains: "I didn't have holidays for four years because I was always involved in these stories. I was so involved, I didn't need holidays, I was inside the real drama, my living was a drama." A passion project tends to be defined as doing something that excites and inspires you, generally (and especially initially) for your own satisfaction, piquing your curiosity, making you go above and beyond the call of duty. Doing work like this can take up all your time, even if it at times involves underpaid or even unpaid labor. It makes journalists vulnerable to exploitation (or simply more agreeable to a less than substantial salary), and less likely to collectively organize and protest. It also makes it much harder to establish boundaries, subsequently making it more likely to take any success and failure quite personally.

JOURNALISM AS A PASSION PROJECT
Corner Media Group (United States)

Having just moved to Ditmas Park in Brooklyn, New York, and studying urban planning, the founder of the Corner Media Group had many ideas and wanted to fix things. Her husband finally pushed her over the edge when she had been walking around with the idea for a hyperlocal blog for a while: "I wanted to make my neighborhood better. That's the simple answer. And once I discovered that, I had readers. I think we had a comment and then all of a sudden we were like oh, people are reading us."

People in other neighborhoods in Brooklyn started doing similar things and they banded together under the Corner Media Group. For the others too, it was important to be able to have an impact in their neighborhoods. By preventing small businesses from closing or getting a dangerous playground sorted, for example: "You won't bring down Nixon or anything like that. But it looks like there's going to be a new traffic safety light going up in the community that's going to make a dangerous intersection safer, partly because of an article I wrote."

It seems enough to keep them going, and makes up for the lack in pay and leisure time. The only times the founder of the Corner Media Group really considers free time are her fishing trips, twice a year, near the Canadian border: "That's my dark time. To go fishing for a week in August. Which is as slow as it is. So, it's whatever. But it's very far away. Eleven hours' driving. There is no electricity, there is no WiFi. It's just peace and quiet."

And that's not even always the case when she goes on holidays: "in two weeks the kids have vacation. So we're going up to Maine skiing. Then my workday will be, you know, get them to ski school, and then work there, and then ... because a lot of it is remote, and so a lot can be done online and does not need to be in person."

The third cornerstone of the interviewees' devotion to the work lies with the emotional quality of the social contacts and the peer community of a collegial environment, which tends to be seen as both *comfortable* (as in providing a sense of well-being, a space where growth can come from) and *comforting* (as in reducing anxiety, and providing relief in difficult times). The social aspects of choosing to start their own company or work for a startup is also mentioned, in contrast to working for established media. A number of the interviewees indicated that they do not find the environment in such companies supportive or inspiring. Such considerations about the emotional environment are important when reviewing their work situation, as this journalist's reflections about a previous job at an established media company illustrate: "they offered me a permanent position, but I ended up declining it, specifically because although there were a lot of good things about the magazine, I couldn't establish a good working relationship with the editor-in-chief."

Interestingly, for the New Beats study, which focused on those who left their jobs, participants' emotional ties with peers and the regular contact with colleagues are things they indicated missing deeply when they switched to freelancing. Some respondents mentioned loneliness; others said they missed the chance to discuss professional questions and issues:

I have questions on my mind, like: which ideas should I pitch to whom and how do I sell them best? Should I invest my time in short-term ideas (pitching to the contacts I already have) or should I aim for long-term development (acquisition to find new clients)?

Given that most studies suggest that the culture of the contemporary newsroom is anything but collegial and friendly, such stories about the working environment are of interest. Reports on conflict-ridden, disorganized, and rivalrous working environments are paramount in the production studies literature – sometimes such a tense context is seen as essential to the creative process of newswork. "This is a competition centered around an ethos which holds that it is right and inevitable to measure one's performance consistently against that of others and that one should thrill in victory and agonize in defeat" (Ehrlich 1995: 208). And indeed, numerous respondents in our survey (as well as those in the other countries where versions of the New Beats study were conducted) would mention this very aspect of newswork as a key motivation to leave the profession. Key here is the emotional quality of the working environment as a benchmark for a reporter's affective investment in the work. If relationships are good and the context collegial, professionals tend to be happier and more willing to engage – whether this concerns a startup, an independent collective, or a more or less traditional newsroom (von Rimscha 2015).

The New Beats project furthermore shows that even when people leave the profession, whether forced or voluntarily, there remains a strong connection with the profession as a whole. Certainly, losing one's job has profound consequences and for most, the profession lost at least some of its luster. At the same time, however, almost none of the participants – nor those in similar studies among laid-off newsworkers elsewhere in the world – are critical of the profession (O'Donnell, Zion, and Sherwood 2016; Heinonen, Koljonen, and Harju 2017; Örnebring and Möller 2018). In fact, 86 percent of Dutch journalists who lost their jobs still feel very positive about the promise and ideals of journalism; 73 percent say that they are proud to be journalists (even if being a journalist is not part of their job description anymore), and two-thirds consider journalism to be a noble profession (Deuze 2019).

This is not to suggest, however, that journalists are without critical concerns about their everyday practice. Indeed, the startup journalists as well as those participants in the New Beats project who have left the profession show a critical engagement with the profession. For the startup journalists it is indeed one of the reasons to go at it in a setting other than established news organizations. And even in their current employment, conflicting sentiments exist. This paradox between a passionate belief in journalism coupled with a profound skepticism toward its practice is powerfully illustrated in this quote of a New Beats participant: "I would not recommend anyone to go into journalism, even though it is the most beautiful profession there is."

With both groups – startup journalists and those who have left the profession – we see that in the main the traditional values and ideals of journalism very much remain the building blocks of their passion for the profession, while its shortcomings tend to be attributed to the way it gets managed and enacted within particular organizational contexts. This continuing loyalty to a "purist" interpretation of journalism and its role in society in the context of a profoundly precarious, at times quite exploitative, and distrusted news industry has been explicitly documented in a study by Nikki Usher (2010) among laid-off US newsworkers. Finding a similar lack of reflexivity connected with a deep nostalgia about what journalism is (or could be), Usher (2010: 923) concludes:

> Significantly, they ... fail to be forward-looking even as they are backward-looking: their nostalgia is self-limiting because it fails to produce a vision of the future that catapults traditional journalists into the new media world and new media economics. Thus, they are limited by their own lack of self-reflexivity and their own sense of loss to see beyond their current situation.

A nostalgia about the "good old days" among newsworkers when faced with job loss and organizational reshuffling was noted earlier in a study of the institutional and cultural contours of innovation at two Dutch newspapers by Sierk Ybema (2003). Ybema typified management strategies in this context as *postalgic*, noting how the industry's executives tend to come up with all kinds of far-reaching plans and futuristic ideals that are primarily interpreted by the journalists involved as unfair criticisms of their work.

However, it seems that journalists embody both nostalgia and postalgia in their ways of giving meaning to their work and career in the context of precarity, professing a melancholic longing for a "better" journalism in the (near) future that simultaneously harks back to an imagined past and future. Whether there is a significant difference, then, between those who have set up shop themselves in a startup or those who have left the profession is difficult to tell, as underneath both their discourses there is a strong identification of what practitioners consider to be the intrinsic value of the profession as a whole. What is striking is how the discourse of the laid-off mirrors the motivations of those starting their own journalistic venture: the profession is beautiful and good – a *passion project* – whereas the way it is managed and how it functions within legacy news organizations is problematic and bad.

This job is beautiful

> This job is beautiful. But you should not accept money because it's the end for you. If you are corrupt, you can't work anymore. You're lost. I'm interested in this job, I'm not interested in money.

What the participants in our research expressed time and time again are variations on the "I can't believe I'm getting paid to do this" discourse popular among creative workers more generally. As found in earlier work interviewing cultural producers, particularly those in new media jobs, these professionals tend to be willing to balance the risk and uncertainty of their jobs against attributes of being part of something fun, exciting, and cool (Neff, Wissinger, and Zukin 2005). Professionals would link perceptions of fun and risk with their distinct personality types, as expressed in numerous instances during our interviews: "this is the most fun I have ever had, and this is most important to me," and "this work is fun and challenging – life is not worth living unless it is fun and challenging. That's kind of my view. And again, part of that is kind of like a personality thing."

This link between startup or entrepreneurial journalism and personality type that the interviewee refers to is articulated in two distinct ways: for one, by suggesting that it takes a certain type of temperament to "make it work" in a new, emerging, and therefore exciting field of journalism, as expressed by this interviewee: "I'm not doing this with the idea that this is important for the world, or whatever. It is just because I thought: if it is possible, I do it. So, it is more because of the challenge." Another way this link gets expressed is by surmising that the way the profession works is addictive: "I'm kind of a journalism addict. I can't stop." Either way, one's commitment to the profession and the particular way of being a journalist within the context of a startup gets internalized beyond questioning: it is simply something you have to do because that is the kind of "real" person you are. This would make it exceptionally difficult to reflect critically on one's predicament, as Bourdieu, for example, suggested: the structural uncertainty that workers find themselves in, he writes, "prevents rational anticipation and, in particular, the basic belief and hope in the future that one needs in order to rebel, especially collectively, against present conditions, even the most intolerable" (1998: 82).

What is specific to startups is the satisfaction derived from a position and status of being on the outside of the established news industry. More often than not, people would describe themselves (and their compatriots) as rebels or rascals on the job, as this particular interviewee does explicitly:

> Yes, I am really happy now. I would not want to go back to an employment contract, to be honest. It is much more fun to be part of this club of young rebels than to be working in a newsroom, I really do not feel like doing that anymore.

The notion of being part of a "club" resonated throughout our interviews, with journalists often referring to their startup work environment as akin to a friendship circle, club, or family: "perhaps it sounds corny but it just makes me happy to start the day together, to work together and also hang out." The reporters at Danish startup Zetland, for example, start the day by singing a song together. Other startups make it a habit to also spend time together outside of work, having cookouts on weekends or even living in the same building (as in the case of some Mídia Ninja editorial collectives in Brazil). In some cases, this social aspect of the work alleviates some of the downsides of working in a highly insecure, generally underpaid context: "so, whatever it lacks in benefits and pay, it makes up for quality of life and office culture and friendship." What makes this a distinct way of talking about the profession beyond the earlier mentioned emotional quality of (doing) journalism is the frame of reference used. The profession tends to be considered as having intrinsic properties that would validate deep investment and belief, which if shared with colleagues can lead to it being a true passion project, whereas the feeling of joining a group, team or club of likeminded, mutually acknowledging professionals also produces (validation for) passionate engagement.

JOURNALISM AS A SOCIAL CLUB
Bureau Boven (Netherlands)

After having graduated from the journalism master's program at the University of Amsterdam, two of the journalists of what later became Bureau Boven decided they wanted to be freelancers, and started looking for a place where they could work together. First at a spare desk at a communications agency of the uncle of one of them – "but we didn't really have anything to do with the rest of the office." Then they joined a small collective of about seven journalists: "we thought that would be fun, also because you are with colleagues there." As the collective grew bigger and bigger, there also came a sense of disconnect: "They were nice and it was fun, but part of them were clearly beta-oriented, science journalists, and the others all worked for women's magazines." So, they went together with a third journalist to start Bureau Boven (which in Dutch means "Office Upstairs," referring to the location of their workspace).

Although the collective started more from the desire for a shared workspace, the three journalists quickly started doing projects together. "I really had the wish to work together again. Not that it was necessary, but I wanted it." That wish to work together is shared by the others: "It may sound silly, but it just makes me really happy to start the day together, to work, and also do things together."

One of them admits there are great projects she would have never done on her own: "You can do these kinds of crazy projects. Alone I wouldn't even get that idea to create an audio tour in Eindhoven – but when you're doing it together you get more and more enthusiastic, and you motivate each other." Finding a lot of social support in each other, they are able to counter some of the downsides they experience of being a freelancer: "It's nice to feel part of something. With a club house, that feeling, that's what you miss when you're a freelancer."

The fun, exciting times had at the startup are set against experiences some journalists have had while working in legacy news institutions, stating how they perhaps wanted the same thing as newsworkers in any context, yet hated the "oppressive" environment there, complaining about a lack of creative opportunities or an overall inefficient way of doing things:

> I want to make money, I want to be successful, I want to be happy. I love not going to an office. I love not taking the subway to work. And not go to meetings. Often that's the number one thing I think about: those meetings.

The generally positive sentiment attached to working like this tends to be explained by referring to oneself as a helpless idealist: "in that sense I am a real romantic and a dreamer. So, the sky is the limit." Beyond such blue-sky thinking (particularly as the vast majority of the startups we investigated were not making any money and could not afford to pay much in terms of a salary to the newsworkers involved), feelings about the job were also considered in a more grounded sense: "it just makes sense, doesn't it, when you're doing what you're most inspired or motivated to do."

Stretching the grounded perspective on working under precarious – yet exciting, even inspiring – conditions further, journalists at times considered the temporal character of the work:

> One thing, I think that's useful to know, is that what I am doing and I think what everyone else is doing in our

organization is, we are doing it because we like it. But it is not that we are going to do this forever.

Realizing that this may not be forever, that working at a startup is quite different from a linear career trajectory at a larger news organization, participants did see beyond the horizon of the next deadline or story: "it is great to create something and then watch it change and be involved in how it grows." Here, a sense of idealism comes back in: "all of this has to do with passion; it is an idealism. You feel that what you do, what we do, is about making sure that this still exists 10 years from now."

Against the grain

> I really did not want to stay there [at an established media company], but liked to freelance. It is just really nice that you have the freedom to write, to make radio and television, that kind of combination of things.

Journalists, like most cultural producers, love autonomy. The freedom to decide what stories to cover, and the freedom to tell such stories in the way they see fit, those freedoms are at the heart of a journalist's professional motivation. Generally, such freedoms are both protected and curtailed in the context of a newsroom at a legacy institution, in that autonomy is restricted by editorial policies, the hierarchical structure of the organization, and the goals of the company. At the same time, the freedom of a reporter to report tends to be guaranteed by the salary, benefits, and social security the company provides, and the same policies that restrict also prevent marketing or other concerns from influencing the work. In a startup environment a lot, if not most, of such structures – clear editorial policies, company guidelines, protections, financial stability, to name but a few – are notably absent. Yet throughout our case studies "freedom" was mentioned as a key motivation to do the work.

Interestingly, a recurring theme within the freedom repertoire was a reference to making, mixing, and thereby also learning, multiple media. Assuming the online environment to be a creative playground, practitioners appreciated the chance to "DIY" their journalism: "I just really want to create a medium where I have control over the information." To put it simply, in the words of one participant, doing journalism means doing "a broad variety of things." In this digital environment the perceived limitations of distinct media would fall away, allowing for some to express themselves differently – something they felt they could not do while employed at a traditional news organization: "I am convinced I can do more. Combine radio, television and newspaper. And the only way to do that is as an independent."

As we have seen before, the experience of working within the context of a traditional newsroom informs the opinions of our participants considerably. Also, within the theme of freedom professionals would agitate against the obduracy of such institutions:

> I find the degree of freedom that I have as a freelancer writer as opposed to being a staffer somewhere also key. People should have the freedom to do whatever they want to do, I think writers should be able to define whatever audience they want.

Sometimes such companies would try to lure people back into the fold – something that was enticing to very few (if any) of the journalists we spoke to:

> Now and then I get job offers and by this time I just immediately say no. I just cannot work in any other way anymore. The thought that every day I would have to sit at some desk at a specific time just kills me. That does not fit me as a person nor my way of life. There is no other way.

As this quote illustrates, here too we find the coupling of professionalism with personality – considering how working within the context of an established news organization supposedly does not fit with the personal inclinations of the independent journalist.

The widely shared reluctance to "go back" to a newsroom job is supported by findings from survey research among freelance journalists. Still, these same studies suggest that most freelance journalists struggle to make ends meet, or have earnings that are not much more than (or fall below) minimum wage (Cohen 2018). Some in our sample equated the freedom they have as an entrepreneurial journalist with financial independence. Several recognized the precariousness of this supposed independence: "I know many that simply cannot handle this level of uncertainty – when is the next assignment? For me this was an advantage because I sincerely enjoyed this kind of freedom." However, all of this freedom comes at a cost, as a significant amount of emotional and material resources need to be dedicated to continuous self-promotion: "well, that was a reason that I felt I did not have the standing nor personality to really represent and sell my work well. On the other hand, writing is my passion."

JOURNALISM AS AN AUTONOMOUS ENDEAVOR
Mediapart (France)

One of the Mediapart founders used to be editor-in-chief at *Le Monde* before he started running the newsroom at Mediapart. He transitioned from a heavy, 300-journalists newsroom with multiple editors-in-chief, producing a print newspaper, to a much lighter, 35-journalists newsroom producing a digital newspaper, and "running the newsroom" has a completely different meaning here. Although he is responsible for making sure that Mediapart is covering the news as well as planning longer term investigations, the organization is much less hierarchical than traditional newsrooms: "you're not in a vertical structure with journalists, then sub-chiefs, chiefs, editors-in-chief, etc. We're in a very horizontal structure where I am, ultimately, together with two colleagues, we're three in total, we're sort of the cockpit of the website."

At the heart of the project is the idea that the journalists will bring their own knowledge, expertise, and passions when they join the startup: "so Mediapart is really a collective dynamic and the journalists have to be completely autonomous and produce their topics and ideas themselves." A journalist working on the education beat at Mediapart indeed feels free to choose her own topics: "That's quite new to me because I've worked at plenty of other newspapers before and this is a place where we're almost completely free."

As the online newspaper could not cover everything, given the small team of journalists, they decided to focus on original stories on a small number of topics. The expertise and professional autonomy of its journalists has been crucial for the success of Mediapart. "We give the journalists as much freedom as possible, because we count on the fact that they will bring us the best topics."

Passion is pertinent in the ways in which our study participants give meaning to the work they do, and this is often related to how they benchmark what they do in relation to established media. In many instances, the journalists involved would emphasize that what they do is "true" or "real" journalism – as opposed to the products "churned out" by colleagues in mainstream, legacy media. Such sentiment was not voiced only by reporters working in societies where the state has a problematically close relationship with the national news media – such as Colombia, Iran, and Nepal. The same criticism about colleagues in legacy media organizations can be heard from startups in The Netherlands, Italy, and the United States. A significant part of the professional identity of the journalists involved with the startups in this study was tied up with perceptions of being "true" to journalism, an ideal-typical and even romantic vision of the profession that in turn legitimized and validated the choices they (individually or collectively in their startup) made. Such dreams of what journalism may be suggest that the ultimate role for journalism in society is to have impact and (thus) make a difference in people's lives (see also the last chapter in this book).

This construction of journalism is not particularly new or innovative. In fact, these reporters and editors would generally refer to a "real" journalism as dedicated to the truth, as functioning as a watchdog, scrutinizing those in power critically and skeptically in the name of the public, and doing so in a way that is professional, transparent, and ethically sound. All of these values can be considered to be the basic building blocks of the consensual occupational ideology of journalism as a profession as it emerged in the twentieth century (Deuze 2005). Still, for the startup workers we spoke with, this ideological vision of professional journalism felt distinct to what they were doing – more often than not suggesting that their counterparts in mainstream media companies somehow had "lost their way" or simply failed society by not living up to their own journalistic standards.

Even though most if not all of the participants were choosing to work outside the traditional system of news institutions, in their discourse they were very much involved with what Matt Carlson (2015: 252) describes as confronting controversy "through the creation of insider–outsider narratives intent on re-establishing the terrain of valid news practices." The controversial terrain in this case, however, is not the outside nor the edge of established news organizations – it is the newsroom and its associated practice that make up the source of contestation or boundary work that journalists do.

In the New Beats research, too, journalists refer to the newsroom as a benchmark, expressing how they experience a higher amount of freedom and independence in their current professional situation, as compared to their previous employment. Yet, they also indicate they are less committed to the media companies and titles they work for (especially the freelancers). At the same time, they feel more engaged with their subjects. As one of the respondents explains:

> Nowadays, I am less likely to see an interviewee as a story for the newspaper. I see them as a person with a story. The fact that I am no longer tied to one particular medium increases my engagement and the satisfaction that interviews give me. ... I feel less like I am playing a role. I meet people as the person that I am, and that feels good.

The real or perceived autonomy our participants touted exists side by side with combining journalistic with more strictly commercial ventures, and also comes with what could be labeled as more "negative" aspects of working outside the organizations. It was not easy to get participants to talk openly about this possibly "darker" side of working independently and being involved with a news startup – such as working all the time (and much of it unpaid). People tended to dismiss potential critical observations and negative experiences as temporary, a passing phase, or a thing of the past – a kind of necessary stepping stone in order to get to a more comfortable position where one would be able to accept (or even welcome) the risk and uncertainty involved. The only time practitioners would be a bit more forthcoming was related to the way they spend their days doing the work of journalism, mentioning how the freedom of their work comes at the price of not having free time anymore: "I really don't know what free time is. I mean, I never really, since I got into this journalism, had free time." They felt they were always working, or expressed that they were still learning on the job how to best manage their time without the structure of a newsroom (with its set working hours, deadline schedules, and production routines). Amanda Brouwers and Tamara Witschge (2019) discuss how such discourse, which normalizes long working hours, is particularly apparent in the combination of journalism and entrepreneurship. In both, working long hours is an accepted norm and startup journalists throughout our sample spoke of these long hours as just part of the job.

Working against the grain for many means cross-subsidizing work, and several of the previously employed journalists in the New Beats project told us that they have adopted a more commercial attitude in their journalism as a result of it. As one of them explains:

> The relation with my clients is entirely about business. I have learned to be distant and not to accept any work before we have agreed on financial compensation. I also work faster than when I was employed. I remember I would spend my free time working sometimes. Today, I still work a lot, but I got better at estimating the maximum amount of time that I should spend on an assignment to make sure it is still profitable.

Journalists who cross-subsidize their newswork with other jobs tend to self-describe their current career and job title as "text writer rather than journalist" or as "half communication worker, half journalist." Similarly, laid-off colleagues in Australia who found new ways of doing newswork in combination with other ways of securing a salary would describe themselves as "partly a journo, but partly something else too" – something that Merryn Sherwood and Penny O'Donnell (2018: 1029–30) consider evidence of a "fading" or "conflicted" professional identity.

Deliberately stepping outside the system of established journalism companies and newsrooms can be both a benchmark and threat for a particular professional identity as a journalist. Although the newsroom job is just as precarious as the independent or startup one – given continuous layoffs and restructuring efforts on the part of management – the added quality for many of having to make it work in as well as outside of journalism can be rather stressful. On the other hand, our participants would often explain away these aspects of the work, instead focusing on their goals, ambitions, and joyous feelings of being involved in journalism this way. It reminds us of Nancy Baym's warning that "we do not have to understand relationships in labor as inherently either genuine or alienating, empowering or oppressive. They are all of these and more, often at the same time" (2015: 20).

For the Greater and Personal Good

Everybody should work like this.

The work that journalists do in general, and being on the job for these startup newsworkers in particular, means so much more than (the promise of) a paycheck or a chance to tell important stories. What we found in our site visits, sit-downs, and interviews was that these practitioners assign certain qualities to their work that are aspirational, both in terms of being professionally as well as socially meaningful and becoming successful on one's own terms. With Brooke Erin Duffy, we consider workers as aspirational (in the way they make sense of being on the job) when they "pursue creative activities that hold the promise of social and economic capital; yet the reward system for these aspirants is highly uneven" (2016: 443). In her interviews with (female) workers in digital media, Duffy found that practitioners would generally discuss their work in three distinct ways: talking about authenticity and realness; highlighting the efficacy of affective relationships (with peers and the community at large); and developing (and devoting oneself to) an entrepreneurial brand identity. These discourses run paramount through our interviews as well, and beget a distinct quality when it comes to journalism.

Regardless of the generally quite creative and unconventional ways these startups conduct their business and manage their organization, most practitioners again subscribe to a rather conventional occupational journalism ideology (Deuze 2005), also when describing the aspirational value of their work: "always exposing. Exposing power. I repeat that many times. Journalists are the watchdogs of power." The notion that journalism has a constitutive role to play in the service of society is paramount, generally defined along basic ideal-typical values such as providing a public service (for the common good), and functioning as a watchdog. These values – framed in the context of what "real" or "authentic" journalism should be about – often got linked to specific goals, such as making a difference and having an impact:

> I don't have a problem with money – I think people should earn money, but what is important is that people are a bit more enlightened. To realize actually I can develop myself as an individual in different ways. One of these things is actually becoming part of society, contributing to society.

Personal and professional goals tend to be mixed up in aspirational narratives, as self-actualization and living up to the ideals of the profession of journalism (especially when set against other communication professions, such as public relations or corporate communication) go hand in hand:

It is funny, just the other day I did a story on Shell and then their press spokesperson asked whether I would want to work there... . But alright, no, I still have my own ethical guidelines, moral compass.

JOURNALISM DRIVEN BY SOCIETAL AND PERSONAL MOTIVATIONS
Follow The Money (Netherlands)

A seasoned journalist with experience at Dutch media such as Quote, the founder created Follow The Money with a clear business model in mind. Firmly believing that media have to "stand on our own two feet," the main challenge was turning investigative journalism into a commercial product.

But when asked what really drives him, he emphasizes the social and personal motivations behind his startup. And even seems a bit uncomfortable with having to "brag" about himself: "We are forced to do that because we want to bring our small brand to the fore. And that's part of it, to say 'hey, look at what we made!' We want to show that. But really, it's actually about the mission. Does a problem become visible through what we do, through our work?"

He criticizes the attitude of journalists who seem more interested in getting their name in the newspaper than they are in the actual story. But doing journalism used to be more about ego for him too. Now, though, he explains his motivations as more "intrinsic." Where he felt like a "gorilla" eight years ago – "hey, look at me, I tackled that asshole!"– he now gets as much pleasure from seeing someone else break a story. The important thing is that the story gets out, not who does it, he explains: "That's not relevant at all to me anymore. It's really about getting things done. And I also really like it when others do that."

Holding power to account through investigative journalism is both a way to serve a societal need and a personal motivation for his work: "I just want to do something I'm good at. That's how I thought about it: hey, I'm good at this, and it is fun."

Hopeful and ambitious statements about one's work must be qualified in the context of precarity – both in terms of working conditions and job opportunities, and regarding the declining levels of trust from the public that journalism enjoys:

> I love good reporters who call it like it is and stand up and point out wrongs. So, I mean, yeah, that part has not changed, I got into it as an idealistic young kid and for some reason now I'm smarter and more mature I realize that's kind of stupid. But for some reason I'm still kind of in that same place. I still think journalism can make the world a better place.

On the other hand, the focus of the profession gets discussed rather exclusively in service of one's own situation and life goals. Such personal goals generally do not include money – nobody we talked with expected to earn much from their newswork – but are more directed toward doing things that are both fun and useful, creative and enjoyable, making a difference as well as helping a professional to get better at what he or she does. This blending of personal and professional goals and explaining away the details of remuneration (or lack thereof) reveal the somewhat particular perspective of the (more often than not unpaid or underpaid) independent newsworker, not beholden to any formal organization – whether that would be a startup, editorial collective, a news business or broadcast company.

Although the journalists we observed and interviewed reflected predominantly in individual terms about their role, motivation, and goals in the profession, this does not mean they feel that they are operating in a vacuum, disconnected from their peers. In fact, quite the opposite: camaraderie and being part of a rather exclusive club were very much at the forefront of their deliberations:

> I really like being part of a club of people who all got into journalism with the same idea, who all want to have an impact on the world with their journalistic work.

This informal "club" of entrepreneurial journalists can also be seen as something akin to a family, both in terms of a potential support structure as well as a context that provides you the freedom to achieve some form of work–life balance:

[Our startup] is one of those companies that you can have a family and still be able to work and support that family. I don't have that family, but it's just one of those places that fosters and supports that.

Here too we see that the aspirational qualities of working for a startup were set against experiences and feelings associated with working in a "regular" job in journalism. References were made to the "pretty abusive office environment" of traditional newsrooms, involving "brutal hours" and generally not being able to do what you want to do. At the same time, we documented how these practitioners described themselves as always being at work and having to combine their passion for doing journalism with making ends meet, selling and promoting themselves and their work constantly in order to stay current, relevant, and (potentially) financially secure. This paradox can be understood by looking at what these jobs mean to these journalists: a club that you belong to, a place within which you can self-actualize, a space where you can be yourself. These meanings provide potent sources of benefit and value to the practitioners involved, which may offset some of the precariousness of working for a cash-strapped startup. Indeed, many professionals would cross-subsidize their newswork with jobs on the side, often on the edges or even outside of journalism.

There certainly is a downside to working like this – doing what you love to do while dealing with profound precariousness. Again, participants tend to see this as "a personality thing," considering it dependent on the kind of individual you are, whether you need or want some kind of security. Security, in this context, can mean a variety of things: the financial security of being able to combine a steady source of income (such as having a weekly column in a magazine or newspaper) with working for yourself and the startup. Security also refers to having individual agency and therefore being able to determine or influence what will happen next – in one's career, regarding the near future of the startup, referring to the development of the profession of journalism as a whole. Additionally, security can be a distinctly social aspect of newswork, when one feels secure in the balancing act between the demands of work and family (particularly with children). The underlying character feature that one apparently needs is flexibility. This is something our participants told us one needs in order to make it work. It is considered to be a specific "quality of life" when choosing to work for a news startup.

You want to be creative

> You want to be able to do two things, right: you want to be creative and also potentially make money. So, I like to be able to be on the ground floor of something that is innovative, something that is possibly breaking through. Being a part of that is exciting, because your handprint is on it. And you get to experiment a lot more and be creative. And you know, people have done something a certain way for a hundred years and you're like: I am going to do it a different way.

The creative and craft-related aspects of the job are a major theme for our research participants. Journalists expressed enthusiasm for being able to do more, to build, and to be involved with something from day one – again, an experience many considered rather problematic or impossible at a more established news organization:

> The ability to present news in a way … You know I couldn't do this at a big media company. They would be like "no, that's not how we do it." But here I get to do it, I get to experiment.

A notion of experimentation and figuring things out as you go along was pervasive in our conversations. Participants felt their days were filled with anything but routine, even at times expressing how being able to consistently calculate and manage their dedicated working hours was something they were not particularly good at. Deadline schedules were seen as never the same and approaches to news were described as determined by the "personality of the site." Regarding individual ways to gather news, one reporter remarked: "Some is just getting the facts, you know a lot of them, almost automatically, almost by a machine. But some things need a little more personal side. And so, it's going to need a personal touch."

Beyond routines and the sedimented working environment, a key complaint regarding established newsrooms was that such office cultures are filled with trappings and, as one participant expressed it, "the whole schmear" of making the organization work: office hierarchies and politics, expectations regarding formal working hours, set deadlines and other structures for decision-making processes, restrictions on the kind of technologies one could use, so on and so forth. In articulating the startup context as having a sense of experimentation and constant renewal, these professionals give credence to a more *liquid* way of working and being at work in an organization, paraphrasing Bauman (2005: 1): the conditions under which its members (workers) act change faster than it takes the ways of acting to consolidate into habits and routines. A liquid context is one in which uncertainty, flux, change, conflict, and revolution are the permanent conditions of everyday life. This is a stressful and high-strung working environment, where boundaries are continuously drawn and redrawn – between work and life, between journalism and other communication work, and between consolidation and experimentation. Workers clearly find solace and value in the various ways of self-actualization that this way of working outside of traditional organizational constraints provides. On the other hand, they have to cope with intense pressures of making it work given precarious incomes and sources of revenue, well-being, reputation, and recognition.

Many of those interviewed for the New Beats project also voice optimistic opinions specifically about (their relationship with) the craft. They appreciate exploring one's creative or experimental urges when it comes to telling stories in new ways and using different media technologies:

> Now I do not have a team anymore and am solely responsible for myself, the whole world of journalism is open for me. Learning new skills, like video, is exciting.

At a 2017 industry conference in Amsterdam we had a chance to discuss this aspect of newswork with Chris Hamby of BuzzFeed and Andrew Golis of Vox. Both emphasized how establishing a culture of experimentation and creativity was key to their organizations' success. Studies suggest that journalists who respond positively to experimentation and innovation tend to be happier and more hopeful at work than those who feel unsure or outright fearful of failure (Ekdale et al. 2015). The challenge, authors note, is to manage such processes carefully. As Hamby and Golis remarked at our meeting, since their organizations started online, they do not have a legacy structure to contend with. This gives them an advantage when trying to establish a culture of experimentation and innovation. Overall, however, the literature is unified in its conclusion that creativity and experimentation tend to be poorly managed in contemporary news organizations (Malmelin and Virta 2016; Ekdale et al. 2015), often leading to skepticism and cynicism among employees. For startup journalists, creativity is a major motivation for being involved in newswork outside of established news organizations, producing tremendous energy and excitement among those we interviewed. They also live experiences of risk and precarity in this way of doing journalism.

4
Making It Work

What we take from our conversations with journalists is a deep appreciation of the paradoxical nature of a professional identity in journalism. To summarize and highlight some of the key contradictions we found in our explorations:

- For many, if not most journalists, journalism is a passion project. A normative sense of *autonomy* is key to their professional identity, while by all accounts the factual (or perceived) autonomy of a reporter today is rather reduced because of the need to self-commodify, to cross-subsidize, and to promote and publish, next to just producing news and information;
- To be part of a *community* of peers, to have a sense of belonging – those are essential elements of making it work for journalists. At the same time, the sociality of journalists on the job can be quite a struggle for many, as the working environment tends to be at least in part based on rivalry, (creative) conflict, and intense competition;
- The enjoyment of journalism as a craft and exercising one's *creativity* is a perhaps understated yet significant element of what it means to be a professional journalist – even if it is generally absent in the common discourse among journalists or poorly managed at the level of the news organization;

- Journalists tend to idealize their profession, as this *ennoblement* is a fundamental feature of their identity – even when the experience of working in that profession can be anything but delightful.

It would be too easy to conclude that the passion of journalists for journalism is what prevents them from having a more critical and reflective view of the profession. Rather, we see that both sense-making narratives coexist: the stories that voice passion and an almost romantic zeal for the profession can coexist with a realistic and at times grim recognition of profound precariousness as a structural feature of job and career. Such narratives do not negate or contradict each other; they even enforce each other at times. The passion story provides fuel for journalists to convince themselves that they can make it work, especially when faced with dire circumstances. At the same time, when the going gets tough, clients and contracts dwindle, and the remaining work consistently gets underpaid, journalists will more often than not blame themselves, articulating a dwindling passion. Critical reflection and passionate engagement sometimes clash, but at other times they coexist independently of each other, taking up different positions in the hierarchy of sense-making tactics and strategies of media professionals. As such, it is important to tell and consider these stories separately, providing insight into prevalent discourses recurring in the conversations with journalists, careful to not fold in (or explain away) one with the other.

To tell the stories of how journalists working outside of established media organizations make it work and make sense of themselves while doing so, we need to understand how these startups are able to survive (and at times even thrive), as often it is at the level of the individual that they make it work. Although we did look at what kinds of products and services the startups in our sample make, our focus here is less on the content than it is on their practice. Relating practice to production, we acknowledge the significant role sources of funding and revenue, as well as (evolving) business models, play in making it work as a startup or startup journalist. Whatever the content being produced, it has to be marketed, commodified, promoted, and sold to an audience – whether that audience consists of news consumers, funders, grantors, sponsors, clients, stakeholders, shareholders, or owners.

Creative accounting

Let us start with the observation that with few exceptions the startups we researched do not earn enough money nor receive enough funding to offset the cost of doing (quality) journalism. There is not a single working business model, as almost all of these small enterprises struggle to make ends meet, and in practice combine several sources of revenue. The competition for attention online, and for grants and other sources of (institutional) funding, is intense, and sources of income and revenue tend to be fickle – often temporary and generally unpredictable.

At the same time, this does not mean these startups are not making it work as businesses. In fact, it has been a revelation to observe the various creative and innovative ways these journalists found sources of income. Denmark's Zetland, for example, sells out theaters with live news performances. Italy's IRPI, on the other hand, employs fulltime staffers who seek out and apply for (international) funding and subsidies. Several startups have membership programs (De Correspondent, Mediapart, Follow The Money), have their finances arranged through public institutions such as universities (MMU Radio, Brooklyn Ink, *Common Reader*), or rely on advertising, sponsored events, paywalls, crowdfunding, subscriptions, donor campaigns, grant income, or some combination thereof.

There are indeed numerous ways to make money in journalism and media. Generally, such business models fall into three categories: a primary, secondary, and tertiary way to make money from a key product or service. With a primary business model, a startup (or even an individual journalist) makes money from producing news. This product can be sold to audiences – for example using paywalls or subscription or membership fees – and to advertisers or sponsors. A secondary business model combines news with a (related) service, for example designing infographics, providing a curation service, or delivering a (syndicated) column for a news publication. Here, the core product of journalism – news – is combined with a related source of revenue in order to make ends meet. Tertiary business models fall in the category of doing what you *have to do* in order to do what you *want to do*. The journalism in this category brings in little or even no revenue at all, forcing the entrepreneurial journalist or startup to provide other services while utilizing their journalistic skills to make it work – such as writing and editing annual reports for businesses, producing catalogues for exhibitions, and providing copy for public relations and marketing campaigns. It becomes clear that the variety of ways to make money in the digital media environment is seemingly endless. This may be so, but handling, organizing, and applying a flexible variety of business models is not easy, nor is it guaranteed to work out.

NEXT LEVEL JOURNALISM
Zetland (Denmark)

At the time of the interview, Zetland had just relaunched six months before and was experimenting with new formats, like podcasts, Zetland Sofa, and comment sections. Their most original format, Zetland Live, was there from the very beginning, combining the Zetland founders' dreams about doing journalism with music and being on stage: "It was a very abstract idea, but that's how it started. Actually, all of us had this dream of being famous, being on stage."

Inspired by *Pop Up Magazine* in the United States, Zetland Live is a biannual event where up to eight journalistic stories each get two minutes on stage: "What we want to do with Zetland Live is to take a paper magazine and take all the aspects from there – notes, essay, interview, all the formats you can find in a magazine or newspaper – and put them on stage." It's a great success; they have done shows for up to 1,500 people and are sold out every time.

Aiming to reach people that are not Zetland subscribers (yet), each year one of the shows is organized with a partner that attracts similar people, like the Danish television show *Deadline* or a vegetable-box company. This responds to a key question that has been on the mind of one of the founders since the beginning: "I kept asking 'how can we make quality journalism and actually make money?' It's easy to quit a job and be an idealist, but that won't last very long if you're not able to make money."

They consider the live shows to be journalism as much as the articles on their website: "It's always nonfiction. I think it's a big misunderstanding that important journalism has to be boring. Because you can do both; we use a lot of effects and things of theaters and music, but the stories are still journalistic stories."

What the discussion of multiple business models in all our interviews and observations signals is the overriding element of "business" running through all accounts of what it is like to work for a startup and making the startup work. Generating funding, income, revenue, and return on investment form a constant factor, permeating all considerations of the work, of living the life of an entrepreneurial journalist. Cross-subsidy (as in the tertiary business model) is something quite common for freelance journalists, as it is for new news organizations. Where a freelance reporter might supplement their income as a journalist with work done for businesses or public institutions, a news company may engage in the production of branded content – producing editorial work that (also) serves as an advertisement for a commercial client. The same is the case in many startups, although quite a few try to either prevent cross-subsidy from happening, or put strict policies in place that would separate marketing and business from editorial decisions. In one case – that of the hyperlocal news network Corner Media Group in New York City – such a policy materialized as a row of potted plants between the advertising section and the newsroom proper.

A fundamental factor impacting people's involvement with these new news organizations is their level of emotional engagement, despite the overall dearth of working business models. As outlined in the previous chapter, journalism is a form of affective labor, in that most journalists tend to choose this line of work for emotional rather than economic reasons, and utilize their emotional capital for professional ends – for example, to feel a sense of belonging, to connect to peers and communities, and to show and use empathy for sources and actors in the news (Siapera and Iliadi 2015). How can we understand the way in which the individual professional relates to the dynamic, uncertain, and unpredictable financial and organizational structures that exist in the field? And how does this individual professional organize their own work on a daily basis? What are the key concerns there? We address these questions in turn.

The networked organization of newswork

Considering the role of journalism in an always-online environment, Van Der Haak, Parks, and Castells (2012: 2927) see the emergence of a new professional figure: the *networked journalist*, whose work is "driven by a networked practice dependent on sources, commentaries, and feedback, some of which are constantly accessible online." They hopefully consider this new role for journalists to be "not a threat to the independence and quality of professional journalism, but a liberation from strict corporate control" (ibid.: 2935). The networked character of newswork gets amplified by a particular feature of the global news industry: the often trans-localized nature of the media production process, as media industries cross-finance, offshore, subcontract, and outsource various elements in the production process to save costs and redistribute risks – most notably the work of foreign correspondents and their teams, especially those operating in conflict areas. A second key element of the networked organization of newswork is its unstable, dynamic, and generally temporary nature – not exactly providing a solid basis for a working business model.

Like media work elsewhere, post-industrial newswork still tends to take place in the offices and on the work floors of specific institutions – including the newsrooms of legacy media companies, but also in the atelier-style offices of editorial collectives and journalism startups, in rented shared workspaces, and in free WiFi café environments as the contemporary landscape of urban media production (Hartmann

2009). As much of this work is contingent, freelance, and temporary, people constantly move in and out of such environments, continuously reconstituting the production process. Furthermore, under conditions of a changing media culture that is more interactive and co-creative (Jenkins 2006), media professionals as well as their audiences are increasingly (expected to be) working together, to converse and co-create. This process accelerates the flow of people, processes, and ideas through the networked enterprise that journalism becomes.

Considering the individualized precarious and networked context of newswork, it becomes imperative to critically interrogate the notion of "organization" as the operational framework for analyzing what it is like to do journalism and be a journalist. In the context of our project, we shift the focus on the behavior of the organization as a macro-structural entity to a perspective on organizations as open systems of interdependent activities, linking shifting coalitions of participants in intra- and inter-organizational networks. In this light, Gernot Grabher (2002) suggests we should not consider the media firm as a coherent and unitary economic actor, but rather consider the enterprise – large or small, newly started or legacy business – as a set of organizational practices that are built around projects, involving a *project ecology* of shifting networks of people from inside and outside the company. In subsequent work, Grabher and Thiel (2015) advocate an additional fine-tuning toward the various impermanent roles played by professionals involved in making projects work – whether this is a major advertising campaign, the multimedia production of a magazine or investigative report, or even the organization of an event.

Looking at temporary projects, teamwork, and networked collaborations enables us to focus on organizations as loosely integrated units of professionals working together – possibly including participants from different disciplines, with different working arrangements and different professional identities, along with collaborating publics. This allows for the equally necessary acknowledgement that much of the work in the media still gets done within the context of observable organizational structures and arrangements. It is this perspective that allows us to both single out journalism startups as discrete and boundaried objects of study within the broader field of journalism as a profession, while at the same time acknowledging how these startups are anything but neatly structured, consistently operational and fixed entities.

Developments in online and digital communication and production and distribution technologies have facilitated the proliferation of many smaller companies and networks able to provide specialized and niche services to the generally more rigid and bureaucratically structured regional, national, and multinational media businesses. This is the case in journalism as in other cultural industries (such as film, television, music, and games; see Deuze and Prenger 2019). In order to make the transition toward a more flexible and networked type of production cycle, media companies in recent years have tended to reorganize themselves into multiple smaller units, or have shifted toward a more decentralized, team-based managerial and working style. This works to flatten existing hierarchies in the company, or to bypass journalism's obduracy – a general resistance to change produced by "routines, practices, and values, developed over time" (Borger et al. 2013: 50).

A key example of the diversified managerial strategy deployed inside news organizations correlates with the emergence of a global startup culture, as venerable news companies create separate divisions or units that function as startups (Küng 2015). These project units tend to have separate budgets, often consisting of members from across (and outside of) the company, and are generally encouraged to adopt a unique, independent workstyle. Their function is as much to inspire the news company as a whole to adopt more flexible ways of working, as it is to develop new sources of revenue and audience attention. In a separate project, Mark worked with three graduate students on case studies of such examples of intrapreneurship in journalism: the Dag6 youth-oriented news app as part of a joint venture between Dutch newspaper Nederlands Dagblad and broadcaster Evangelische Omroep, the MediaLab of Dutch public broadcaster VPRO, and the Digital Story Innovations team at the Australian public broadcaster ABC. Combining site visits, observations, interviews, and document analysis, we found that these attempts at creating a startup environment within legacy media organizations primarily function as examples of what Tanja Storsul and Arne Krumsvik (2013) call *process* and *position* innovation. The intention here is mainly to innovate the way stories get told (for example by establishing teams where journalists, data analysts, and designers work together), or how the news product gets positioned in the market (by deliberately targeting a younger, online-only audience).

The way of working of these intrapreneurial outfits was rather unusual (often much more networked, without a fixed working space or daily structure, making things up as they went along), and the composition of the teams constituting them very different (much more interdisciplinary, including marketing and design professionals next to reporters and editors) than the traditional newsroom. However, in terms of producing content, these cases did not necessarily differ all that much from what their colleagues elsewhere made. A key insight from these cases is the recognition of how a new organization of newswork does not necessarily produce a different kind of news.

Whether started on the outskirts of the news industry or in the very heart of the contemporary newsroom, new journalism ventures, initiatives, and pilots are coming into being everywhere, adding to the already dynamic nature of the profession and pushing its professionals to broaden their skillset and take on more responsibilities. It is within this context that a global startup culture has developed, both within and outside of traditional newsrooms. It is important to note that despite many changes within traditional newsrooms and many new players operating outside the newsroom, the newsroom has not become obsolete. Quite the contrary – we argue that to understand startup practices of work, we need to understand the newsroom.

(Re)visiting the newsroom

If we take the starting point that in many ways the newsroom and its specific organization of newswork is still important – in fact is key to understanding what contemporary journalism is – we can first ask what we see inside newsrooms located in a legacy media organization. For one, we would observe a lot of empty chairs. The number of layoffs in journalism – especially in print – has been astounding over the last decade. Reports of journalism unions and professional associations such as the Media, Entertainment and Arts Alliance in Australia, the Society of Professional Journalists in the United States, the National Association of Journalists (NVJ) in The Netherlands, and the National Union of Journalists in the United Kingdom in recent years suggest that their members see their colleagues being fired and not replaced. Journalists working in newsrooms consistently report having to do more with fewer colleagues, lower pay, and less resources. Long-term planning and advancement (in terms of "moving up the ladder" within a newsroom hierarchy) have been replaced by job-hopping and a portfolio work life, as news professionals increasingly have (temporary, contingent, casual) contracts, not careers in journalism. As a consequence, stress and burnout are on the rise among newsworkers, with many journalists considering leaving the profession altogether (Reinardy 2009 and 2011; Cohen 2018). Precarity and a culture of job insecurity have come to define the lived experience for many inside the contemporary newsroom (Ekdale et al. 2015).

Of the people who are left in the newsroom proper, some still enjoy permanent employment (including benefits and protections). These (generally senior) staffers work side-by-side with a host of colleagues in part-time, contract, freelance, temporary, flexible, and at times underpaid or unpaid roles such as interns: professionals who come in irregularly to file stories, produce segments, push stories online, or provide other editorial services (Cohen 2015: 515). But not only these contractual working arrangements of newsroom colleagues are underrepresented in discussions of the profession (about itself) and, subsequently, in surveys and ethnographies of news organizations: the myriad of additional workers in the newsroom, ranging from technical support staff, copy editors, ombudsmen and reader representatives to designers, producers, and programmers, are often left out of the conversation too. In recent years, however, such functions have multiplied in the newsroom with the emergence of new roles and positions and they are increasingly important in shaping the practice, output, and distribution of journalism.

Permanent jobs are scarce, and generally unpaid internships and other forms of free or underpaid labor now determine access. All this is accompanied by a rising cost of entry into journalism: a trade school diploma is a bare minimum – for jobs in the (national) quality news media, in practice a high-level university education is required. Student grants have been cut, their duration shortened, or they have been converted into loans. The majority of newcomers in the profession start as self-employed journalists. Tariffs for freelancer journalists have declined over the past decade. To use The Netherlands as a particular example: not only has freelance remuneration declined (up to 50 percent for news photographers), almost half of Dutch freelance journalists today depend on the income of their partner, and about half cannot make ends meet with their newswork (based on national representative surveys conducted annually since 2016; see Vinken 2017). Interestingly, 70 percent of these independent newsworkers prefer this way of making a living over having a permanent salaried position in journalism.

Careering journalism?

The ways in which newswork is organized affect news as an institution; they also affect individual career trajectories. Peterson and Anand (2004) suggested that careers in the fragmenting and casualizing media industries tend to follow two different paths. The first is a top-down career, largely established through lifelong participation in vertically structured institutions, where seniority, experience, and a transparent system of salaries guide the professional toward higher positions in the office hierarchy, resulting in more or less permanent positions within the newsroom. In more competitive environments where the organization of work is tailored toward flexible production, "careers tend to be chaotic and foster cultural innovation, and career-building market-sensing entrepreneurs enact careers from the bottom up by starting from the margins of existing professions and conventions" (Peterson and Anand 2004: 317). Today, a third trajectory can be added: the *patchwork career* (Michel 2000) of the atypically employed individual finding his or her permanence in impermanence, forever flexibilized, whether on the outside or the inside of news institutions.

Newsrooms are still creating positions, yet often these are temporary structures designed as informal internships, often with little pay. Moreover, the new jobs that are available in journalism tend to be in the digital domain (including more technologically focused jobs), and do not make up in numbers for layoffs elsewhere in the news business. With the accelerating dynamic of reorganizations and reshuffling, buyouts and layoffs, new owners and managers, new work arrangements and budget cuts, journalism has become more precarious and less accessible to everyone. In fact, if we put it provocatively, it increasingly seems to be the playing field of only those who can afford to work for years or even for the majority of their careers below or around the minimum wage in the largest and therefore most expensive cities, as that is where the main news outfits (as well as most hyperlocal companies and news startups) are generally located.

Beyond the dynamic, often-changing, and precarious business model of the various startups, in this project we ask how professionals beyond journalism give shape and meaning to their careers. With the growing precariousness of newswork and the rapid rise of freelance, independent labor and self-employment, what is the quality of people's patchwork careers? Such questions range from the basics of paying the bills (and possibly supporting a family) to broader issues related to the management of risk and coping with uncertainty.

The question of careers in journalism is a fascinating one. As much of what we know about journalism (and what journalists perceive journalism to be) is derived from the discourse and process of professional socialization within established news organizations, we wonder how independent journalists develop a coherent sense of professional identity in the context of networked journalism. We found that many of the journalists we spoke with combined their startup activities with other work; this is a clear signal of how the precarity intrinsic to "making it work" in journalism stretches across the in/out boundary between legacy and startup companies. Furthermore, many journalism startups are in the business of generating stories, raw materials (i.e., research), products and services to be sold to legacy news companies. In so doing, these independently employed newsworkers are never far away from the traditional industry outside of which they position themselves.

In the New Beats project, much like in the interviews with the startup journalists, we found that the trajectory toward a stable career and professional identity in journalism is quite complicated. Key elements that give a journalist's career trajectory meaning – working autonomously, being part of a peer community, honing your craft, and playing out your passion for the profession – can be internally quite contradictory, particularly given that those participating in the New Beats project (in contrast to the startup journalists) also indicated valuing "security" as an important element in their career, especially after experiencing the loss of a job in journalism. Overall, we find that the "career" beyond journalism is anything but stable and coherent – instead, it is something best understood as "permanently impermanent" (paraphrasing Bauman 2005: 33).

The occupational identity of journalists working under conditions of networked journalism comes closest to that of artists, whose status is similarly ambiguous. Artists also operate in largely unregulated, uncharted contexts (Kosmala 2007: 37). Like artists – whose work often is unpaid or underpaid, relying on unpredictable sources of (financial) support, and who tend to work in informal arrangements – the construction of an occupational identity for entrepreneurial journalists takes place using shared myths about what it is like, and what it should be like, to be a professional. Both the senior reporter being laid off after a long career in the news industry, as well as the junior journalist joining a startup, frame their work and career in mythical terms, such as the need to be autonomous, the significance of the craft, and their belief in the power of the profession to matter and make a difference in society.

What is interesting is how the professionals we talked with coupled such traditional notions of journalism with an enthusiasm for creativity, innovation, and doing things differently (or completely anew) as key elements of how they give meaning to their work. This almost romantic idea of what (startup) journalism is or should be seems quite similar to what Gregory Feist (1999) considers the defining feature of what it means to be an artist in contemporary society: a tendency to rebel against established norms by questioning, challenging, and defying the limits of acceptability. In her work on how artists construct an identity, Alison Bain (2005: 34) signals how "to be a professional artist, then, essentially involves successful claim and defence of professional status through the construction and maintenance of an artistic identity." In doing so, Bain highlights three issues shaping the occupational identity of the artist:

- The significance of being part of a community (which confers recognition, a sense of belonging, as well as mutually establishing the legitimacy of what you are doing);
- The significance of working freely, as a matter of personal choice, and being creative (which enables practitioners to accept the precariousness of their careers, while it constrains efforts to do something about this precarity – as freedom, choice and creativity are attributes that most people generally associate with leisure activities rather than salaried work);
- The significance of "the art of compromise," as practitioners tend to have to supplement their income from art with secondary employment, something we see throughout our cases and studies with reporters cross-subsidizing their work (often including gig work in marketing communications or public relations contexts).

FUN, FREEDOM, AND CHALLENGING
Freelancer *Alaska Dispatch News* (United States)

Switching careers from personal training to journalism, a "natural passion" for hiking came in handy: "Obviously I didn't have any clips to my name. All I could say was 'I'm a really good hiker and I'd like to write about it'."

As a child, the freelancer dreamt of working for publications like nationwide *Alaska Magazine* or the *Milepost*: "I could see the *Milepost* camper from outside of my window and I know it might not appeal to a lot of people, but to my personality the idea of just being paid to sort of hobo around the state very much appeals to me."

Although she doesn't really mind that every hike is now a potential story, she did stop writing for fun: "I make it a point to do nonwriting things. I have fun when I write, but I'm writing for work. And I have fun."

At the same time, she experienced how it's not only fun and freedom as a freelancer. Going through a very difficult personal situation a few years ago, she realized that being a staffer would've helped her deal with it more easily. Such issues can affect your work much more when the lines between private and professional life get blurred: "The issue was that there was nobody but me to impose a framework on me." She almost worked herself into the ground.

Still, it's worth it, she explains: "to do what makes me happy, having the freedom to say this doesn't make me happy today, so I'm doing this instead." And it helps that she can physically close the door of the office now that she has a three-bedroom townhouse: "I never had a physical barrier to my workplace. In the studio apartment I just had a corner of the apartment that was my dedicated office."

Journalists may consider their profession a passion project – it is clear that beyond that ideal they also simply have to make it work on a day-to-day basis. We would therefore like to suggest that a more grounded way to understand individual journalists' relation to journalism is how they *achieve a workstyle* rather than *build a career*. Achieving a workstyle that fits does not come easy in the precarious environment in which journalists work, and we next consider some of the tensions that came up in the conversations with the research participants.

Achieving a workstyle

The contemporary career, especially when considered in the context of a global startup culture and the rise of the networked journalist, needs to be seen in terms of a more or less ongoing process of achieving a workstyle. People's efforts and energy go into developing a blend of work and lifestyle: a workstyle, where life becomes a way of *working* and a way of *being at work*. For one, this means that people are always at work, as one reporter looks back: "I did not have holidays for four years. I did not need holidays." Beyond a holiday, one wonders about what is left of a distinction between work time and free time. "Free time? Ehm, you mean in my life? I don't know, I guess the weekends. I have free time, at night. I don't know. I have two children so I don't feel like I'm really free. So, the weekends. I don't really know."

The professionals invariably refer to their workstyle as something they achieve on a day-to-day basis, without necessarily succeeding in establishing some kind of rhythm, structure, or routine. "My grandfather worked as an analyst in a company. He always says 'yes, just structure your time.' That is impossible, it definitely does not work like that." Some would attribute this quality of working and being at work to the distinct nature of a startup environment, as this journalist reflects on what it means to work for a startup:

> That was actually really hard, that was another thing that I knew it was a startup, we were all doing very long hours, because we knew we had to maintain the site and we had to keep on top of the news as best as we can. That was another thing, editorial selection. We couldn't write everything, every story, just because we didn't have enough people. That was another way I knew [I was working at a startup].

It is hard work – but that is not all it is, participants stress. They would mention working on their workstyle, trying to figure out ways to bring more balance to their everyday lives. Often, they would seem to actually enjoy this process. "My day is kind of weird. In the middle of the day I go to the gym – when there is nothing crazy going on – and then I continue in different meetings. On the weekends, I have free weekends, it's not like work all the time at all." Similarly, while juggling work with a family, the freedom an independent or startup context provides is heralded:

The nice thing about [our startup] is that, I have children, I can pick them up, take out two hours of the working day and make them up later. So, I can respond to e-mails at ten at night, but I can get an e-mail at six in the morning and also respond. It's very fluid.

"IT NEVER STOPS"
InkaBinka (United States)

The only time when one of the InkaBinka editors is not available is when he's at the gym. But then the other editor – his sister – knows that she needs to be extra alert. When asked what he considers "free time," the editor responds: "I go to the gym every day and usually I don't bring my phone with me. But I'm only there for an hour... . That's probably the only time when I am not doing work."

Although editing a story for the automated news tool only takes a few minutes, he feels he has to be "on" all the time, and will even work during social gatherings: "Most of the people that I'm with know that this is what I do. So they understand that I have to, you know, attend to work at any moment, at any given moment. And it's become ... it's sort of not that difficult anymore. I just press pause on what I'm doing."

At the time of the interview, his sister had just started another job at a radio station. "But it's just going to be a weekend thing," she assures, and it might even be beneficial for her InkaBinka work: "I'll be doing a lot of the board switching stuff and there's going to be a good amount of down time, so during that down time I'll just edit. And I would be up early ... earlier ... so it will be good for editing also, haha."

Working with your sister for a company founded by your father makes the boundaries between professional and personal lives less clear: "it's very much a part of the entire family. So, every time there's a family gathering, it comes up in conversation. And it's hard to keep it out of the conversation usually."

Still, the founder treats his children as he would any other employee: "They actually have to perform. They don't ask for favors because they know they won't get them."

The workstyle becomes something to achieve in real time, all the time. As we have seen when considering the nature of the job in a startup environment, responsibilities of job and family, leisure time and work time, establishing some kind of routine and being flexible are anything but stable and are constantly renegotiated. Interestingly, participants would see this as particular to their career choice as being independently or self-employed, considering this an unpredictable feature of work while at the same time emphasizing this as an element of freedom. In achieving their workstyle and making it work, three themes continuously came up in our conversations with the participating journalists: striking a balance between freedom and some sense of security; the necessity to cross-subsidize newswork; and figuring out how to cope with stress and uncertainty.

Freedom versus security

Security and autonomy tend to coalesce in professionals' view, as being (or feeling) financially and professionally secure. However, security in any traditional sense – as in having a salary, being able to afford healthcare, providing for a pension – is largely absent for these startup reporters and editors. This is a double-edged sword, as participants alluded to:

> This is naturally quite dependent on the individual, what kind of need for security you have. I know many who really cannot deal with this level of uncertainty – when is the next assignment or paycheck coming? For me, it was an advantage, because I really enjoyed this level of freedom.

The flexibility one needs to make a career work in a precarious predicament puts permanent pressure on the workers, but it does confer some sense of autonomy in the face of the news industry: "I have a lot of flexibility, which is great. I like the freedom to be able to do what I want to do, to build a schedule of things." Certainly, careers like this are partly built on a social support structure:

> Doing journalism in this way is generally not so good for one's private life, you just have to coordinate all of this and

friends and family need to understand. I do not think it makes much difference whether you have a permanent contract or being self-employed. It depends how you make it work.

Although our participants would rarely, if ever, refer to their social environment (other than the co-workers in the startup, and only sometimes mentioning they have children), clearly the choices they make in this career affect the people they live and work with in a profound way.

In the New Beats project, a frequently mentioned concern and consequence of a layoff is a decline in income and resulting financial insecurity. On average, the Dutch respondents who are working in journalism earn less than they did before their contract was ended or expired – a situation mirrored in the experiences of recently laid off Australian journalists (Zion et al. 2016). Particularly the female journalists now earn much less than they did before. One of the participants in The Netherlands describes the situation:

> After four years of struggling in a country that is not cheap, I am not sure how long I can persevere. I don't manage to save up money. If I would have a client who would pay a fixed fee every month, that would give me peace of mind. But all my clients pay per contribution. That provides me a huge amount of freedom, but gives a feeling of restlessness too. I haven't managed to find the right balance yet.

For those over sixty years of age, redundancy causes less concerns – it even gives some the chance for early retirement. Worries do prevail among younger reporters: about pension shortfall, loss of financial security, termination of collective healthcare provisions and other insurances, and about lack of equipment that they had available with their former employers. Furthermore, professionals point out that they feel more insecure about their future in general. Back on the job, one journalist remarks: "Much more than before I feel like I am fair game." This can have problematic consequences, as workers stop voicing their opinions (for example about certain projects, innovations, or other managerial interventions) in order not to be seen as a "difficult" colleague:

> For the sake of job retention, I tend to be more cautious
> when communicating with my superiors. I am hunting for
> new opportunities and make sure not to push issues too hard,
> because I don't want to risk losing my job.

The factual or perceived lack of opportunity and freedom to
voice concerns (or opposition) within the news organization
is found in other studies as well. Interviews with Israeli
journalists, for example, suggest that major news organizations in their country are seen as riven by internal conflict and
characterized by a management deficit, which dysfunction
contributes to practitioners' problems voicing discontent
(Davidson and Meyers 2016: 597). It may be that the lack
of job security in startups offsets the professionals' desire for
more freedom – to express themselves and to give shape to
the kind of journalism they aspire to.

Cross-subsidizing work

As most freelancers or self-employed reporters have to cross-
subsidize in order to earn a decent living, the ability to network,
build and maintain good relationships, and convert contacts
into clients are necessary building blocks to a career. Mixing
and matching different kinds of journalistic work, combining
it with non-journalistic work, and juggling the demands (and
pursuit) of different clients can be daunting tasks:

> I was writing ... columns; that's how I got started. So, I did
> that for about three years and worked part-time retail jobs
> to make ends meet. I'm not sure if I was moonlighting as a
> journalist or moonlighting as a retail clerk. I'm not sure what
> way that worked.

Wearing different or even multiple hats also comes into focus
beyond the particulars of a freelance career, as journalists
with contracted employment (at startups or in jobs that would
support the work they are doing for a startup) also are facing
pressures to combine the responsibilities of newsgathering,
writing, editing, and producing stories with publicizing and
promoting the work. As part-time and temporary contracts

are the norm, moving from one title to the next, often from one medium to the next, becomes a regular feature of one's job-hopping career trajectory:

> Today I have a story in a magazine. I'm starting at a hyper-local news startup, I write columns for another magazine, and I just completed a three-day stint at a radio station. This is the real journalist life, I guess.

Quite often one's work for a startup or within an editorial collective tends to be something a journalist would do on the side of their regular work – whether that would be a job in journalism or something else entirely. Examples mentioned prominently: running a photography or videography business (for hire), doing training and consulting work, and writing copy for a variety of businesses and organizations.

Several interviewees indicated that they would continue to be involved with their startup even if they got a job offer from an established news organization; they would opt to combine that work. The art of combining clients, contracts, assignments, and appointments is a delicate and consuming one, generally leading to periods of frenetic activity when money flows in:

> I try to combine a lot of things. For example, if I succeed in getting some kind of big grant, I will produce a lot of stories, reports, and documentaries in a couple of weeks, back to back. Then I'll try to find as many different channels as possible to sell this work to.

The bottom line is that, generally speaking, working for a startup and doing freelance newswork generally pays poorly. As one participant says: "it still feels like a hobby that got a little out of hand. So yes, that produces stress sometimes."

Although cross-subsidizing can add up to a decent annual income, the discussions we and our students had with the journalists were at times quite intense. Journalism is still seen as the ultimate profession and its craft as the ideal. This quest for purity – of simply wanting to "get the damn story and get it out there" as one reporter exclaimed – at times banged up against the necessity of dealing with the nitty-gritty of running a startup organization, such as attending meetings and making business decisions. The clearest notion of the quest for a journalistically "pure" career came in discussions about the economics of it all. Few journalists mentioned comfort in combining their reportorial work with (jointly or independently) managing a company, with some exceptions:

> I have always been kind of a hustler growing up, I always had jobs when I was a kid going around the neighborhood trying to make money, things like that. I guess I always had a drive, in that sense. But the business sense just came as I went through trial and error and reading a lot and learning from others and asking others.

Robert Picard (2010) has suggested that the professionalization of journalism – leading to journalists generally enjoying unprecedented autonomy in their work – simultaneously separated journalists from business decisions and removed them from any responsibility for the organization's actions and sustainability. From our interviews it is clear that, while startup founders, editors, and reporters were keenly aware of the precariousness of their business and the need to contribute to its sustainability and growth, many felt this came as a detriment to what they really want to do – which is doing good journalism.

Coping with stress

Passion can be a beautiful thing – and it also can get you into trouble. Doing what you love makes everything you do very personal, making it hard to maintain boundaries (between work and life, for example). As these journalists dive head over heels into their work, they subject themselves, their careers, and their loved ones to intense periods of activity that more often than not come with a range of stressors: working overtime, meeting deadlines, securing financing, trying out new things without any assurances it will work, working without well-established structures for feedback and support... For some of the cases in our sample one should add to these stressors those of working in restrictive or repressed media cultures (such as Iran, Nepal, and Colombia), as well as overcoming infrastructural problems of distribution. In the case of the weekly children's news television program *Naya Pusta*, for example, this meant navigating the mountainous terrain of Nepal and managing the work during and after the earthquake of April 25, 2015:

> Since the geographical structure of Nepal is very difficult, while going outside the valley. It's really difficult. Our vehicle can't go there and we need to work. It's difficult because of the geographical situation and besides that, after the earthquake, after the big earthquake, the situation was really difficult. It was really difficult to work. The day when the earthquake came, we were working in the field. And it became really, really difficult for me to work.

Beyond such problems, the average startup has to work hard at promoting and publicizing their work to get people to see the content, as most rely on their own publication platform. Many offer a distribution mix of getting the work on air or in print at established news services, putting it up on their own website, and reselling it for third party use. With the absence of entrenched models for working like this, figuring things out on the fly can be quite stressful, as this quote illustrates:

> We kind of wandered into an area where nobody in our country has been before. And that makes it special and really fun. It is also really exciting and tense, so that it sometimes keeps you up at night, when things go wrong.

Another fundamental feature of a potentially stressful career path for these newsworkers is the lack of revenue, salary, and pay characterizing most of the startups we looked at:

> Also, somehow, I have to secure a specific sum of money, even though I simply do not want to work myself to death. There are always projects and things get really intense and stressful, where I work day and night for a month or so, after which I need a break.

The third source of stress for our journalists was time – or the lack thereof. As noted, work has spilled over into all other domains of life, and the feeling of working all the time can be both exhilarating and draining. It becomes stressful to just keep on going, to combine work time with family time, to constantly rearrange one's schedule because of the unpredictable nature of the job and career.

Personality matters

What becomes clear from our interviews, with both startup journalists and those whose jobs recently ended in legacy media, is that journalism is as much a *passion* project as it is also a highly *precarious* project for the professionals involved. And much like the discourse on journalism as passion project, those discussing journalism as *precarious* suggest that it takes a certain type of personality to be able to work like this. As several participants suggest: "yes, journalism is something of a ... not selfish, but it suits our own curiosity, obviously. You have to have a certain personality for it." Journalists feel that it takes certain qualities that make up the "right" character to work in journalism generally, and as an independent worker specifically.

Specific personal characteristics mentioned are (a restless) curiosity, extraversion, being flexible and sociable, and most of all being able to "thrive with the right amount of instability" (as one interviewee put it). It is debatable whether any of these characteristics are unique or exclusive to working for a startup, but the journalists we spoke with generally associated their personalities with this singular career choice. The uncertain and unruly nature of the startup would, for some, fit their private life perfectly as well:

> I'm an extravert, you know when you take that personality test, I'm extreme to that, so I need to be around people all the time. And my general life is really loud and chaotic all the time, I have a big family, I have children crazy, all of that, so I think that like a baseline of warmth in camaraderie, for me it's a comfortable place to be. And I don't like to be completely solitary. It helps me to stay on task to be around other people.

For others, the same situation would provide them with the freedom to withdraw: "I don't think my personality is the most outgoing ... I like to stay behind the scenes and behind the screen [more] than take the front stage. And you know, the others can take the front stage and go to meetings."

In general, it is once more testament to the emotional nature of labor in creative contexts such as (beyond) journalism that workers would consider their personality as a fundamental element sustaining this kind of work and giving meaning to being at work. With David Hesmondhalgh and Sarah Baker (2011), we ask how personality matters in these creative careers both as a way to *enjoy* the profoundly precarious context of working, as well as to *self-police* the stressful and intense ways of being at work. One's personality – being sociable and outgoing, for example – contributes to disciplining oneself when faced with the inevitable conflict that arises in creative work environments where there is little or no privacy and informality is prized over strict office protocol. Also, dealing with the pressures of "making it work" for both yourself as well as the company requires a fair amount of emotional labor, having to stay on good terms with colleagues and clients, the community, as well as (potential) sources and authorities.

Journalists working within and outside of the traditional newsroom environment are finding making their careers work to be complicated. For some, this means hunkering down, just doing the work and staying out of sight next time some managerial innovation is proposed or a company overhaul is introduced. Others strike out on their own in an act of resistance. They sometimes meet in intrapreneurial or entrepreneurial settings – at in-house innovation outfits or standalone startup businesses. Whatever their chosen path, making it work for these reporters and editors involves a fair amount of financial, economic, and emotional acrobatics. What gives all of this meaning is not just an affective commitment to the work and the profession – it is also a sincere conviction that (good) journalism truly matters.

5
Stories that Matter

In this project and book, we have followed a pragmatic definition of who is a startup journalist. Beyond focusing on practitioners who deliberately operate next to or outside of legacy media institutions – and who consider themselves journalists – we have not concerned ourselves much with setting up a rigorous definition of "journalism" at the basis of our work or sampling strategy. The protagonists of the stories told in this book have been selected by sheer excitement, interest, and fascination of our students and us. Our project follows the path of a comparative case study design, in that it aims at understanding rather than generalizability – it is a holistic rather than a reductionist approach (Verschuren 2003). Although this does not make the various startups, entrepreneurial initiatives, and collectives profiled in this book a generalizable sample, the longitudinal multiple case study design of the project meets our goal of highlighting multiple stories and embracing divergent perspectives of what journalism is (or could be), rather than suggesting that there is a particular story that is representative of the field at this time. As Thomas Wrona and Markus Gunnesch (2016: 727) articulate, it was important to our team to do research with the explicit aim of increasing the number of possible interpretations – expanding what they call the "repertoire to interpret."

At the same time, operational definitions are at play, and are important here. The term "entrepreneurship" has become increasingly prominent in how policymakers, industry observers, professionals, and scholars understand media work in general, and newswork in particular. While journalism has for a long while been understood as a practice deeply embedded in institutional structures (as exemplified by the newsroom), we have witnessed a significant shift in journalism education, critique, and practice in which the future of journalism is envisaged to (also) lie in a "de-institutionalized" or post-industrial profession practiced by a variety of free agents, entrepreneurial journalists, and otherwise atypically employed newsworkers (Burns and Matthews 2017; Creech and Nadler 2018). To understand entrepreneurship as an answer to the transformations in the news industry toward a networked style of production is not isolated to the field of media: it is a perspective much in line with a broader trend to see entrepreneurialism (and even more specifically the "enterprising" individual) as a solution to societal problems. Audretsch (2007), for example, speaks hopefully of an "entrepreneurial society" as a supposedly optimal society where everyone is an independent entrepreneur, seeking self-employment and self-fulfillment, all the while confidently surfing on the seas of constant change.

Understanding the future of journalism through the lens of "entrepreneurial journalism" is not neutral or unambiguous – it favors a particular form of journalism, a form that we should question for its precarious basis and its blindness to systemic critique. It also considers the future of journalism within a very narrow frame, in which innovation and change in journalism are considered strictly in terms of economic and technological solutions, rather than considering media technologies and work as constitutive of social innovation (Podkalicka and Rennie 2018). What we found particularly inspiring in our observations and discussions with the research participants is their heartfelt commitment to social change and improving the lives of communities. In this final chapter, then, we consider first the particular discourses of entrepreneurship used by our interviewees, and what kind of issues these raise. Second, we consider what the journalists we talked with aim for with their entrepreneurship: how do they think about their own role in shaping the journalistic field, and how do they define journalism that matters?

Beyond definition and tradition

Definitions, concepts, and the "metaphors we live by" (Lakoff and Johnson 1980) affect the actual practices of the people whose stories we document in this project. As Lakoff and Johnson (1980: 3) explain, definitions are not neutral:

> The concepts that govern our thought are not just matters of the intellect. They also govern our everyday functioning. Down to the most mundane details. Our concepts structure what we perceive, how we get around in the world, and how we relate to other people... . the way we think, what we experience, and what we do every day is very much a matter of metaphor.

Entrepreneurialism, as a concept in our project, neither follows nor provides an ultimate definition of who is (and who is not) an entrepreneur in journalism. If anything, the entrepreneurial mindset – being willing and able to take risks, seize opportunities, and embrace change – is something very much part of any journalist's repertoire for survival, whether working in a salaried, contracted, or atypical capacity. We are primarily interested in how our interviewees describe what it is that they are doing, as entrepreneurs, and what journalism in that context means to them. As having an impact and doing journalism that makes a difference clearly matter to the study participants, we wonder what kind of space for agency and opportunity these reporters see to create the kind of practice and product that they believe is valuable. In raising such questions, we do not look for the particular traits and personality characteristics of entrepreneurs. As pointed out by William Gartner in 1989, such an approach would "neither lead us to a definition of the entrepreneur nor help us to understand the phenomenon of entrepreneurship" (48). We want to know what being an entrepreneur means to our interviewees, how this is embedded in the social context of running a (new) company, and how this translates into doing work that matters – which in turn contributes to the reshaping of journalism.

Research has shown that startups, as a particular form of entrepreneurial journalism, abound (for a review of the landscape in Europe, see Bruno and Kleis Nielsen 2012; for Australia, see Simons 2013; for some US cases, see Schaffer 2010 and Coates Nee 2014). At schools and programs in journalism education around the world, correspondence courses and degrees in entrepreneurial journalism are developed (Vázquez Schaich and Klein 2013; Mensing and Ryfe 2013). Academic research is also devoted to this area, focusing on startups (Vos and Singer 2016; Powers and Zambrano 2016; Usher 2017), individual entrepreneurs (Fulton 2015), as well as editorial collectives (Rodrigues and Baroni 2018). If much or at least part of the future of journalism is deemed to lie in entrepreneurship, what then do we talk about when we talk about entrepreneurship? Our interviewees name a lot of different things when they explain what entrepreneurialism is for them. For some it is starting from scratch, as these two quotes explain:

And so, it really started in January 2007, but everything still had to be done at that point. We had no technology experience in the digital domain and no entrepreneurial experience.

I knew it was a startup because the whole first week of my work was producing content that was not going live. It was running through the systems, testing things.

The act or feeling of treading new ground, of venturing out into unfamiliar territory, makes them consider themselves as entrepreneurs. This is a common way to understand entrepreneurship. Whereas journalism as a profession is generally more associated with routines and conventions, bound by tradition (see also Witschge 2013), entrepreneurship is often considered as its opposite: breaking new ground versus accepting the status quo. It is a sense of adventure that attracts certain people to join new journalism enterprises. Entering this new environment, trying out new ideas, gets connected to the notion that as an entrepreneur you need to be "daring" and able to let go of control to a certain extent, as this quote illustrates:

You make the wrong decision often and the best cure for the wrong decision is to fail fast. To be able to recognize that because people get emotionally attached to their ideas and they don't want to let them go. But you need to be able to let that idea go.

In our interviews, entrepreneurship gets expressed with a discourse of "bravery" that includes references to going above and beyond the call of duty in order to make it work:

We don't have enough crazy young people like [the person running the startup]. It takes, you know, you have got to be really committed. Like I said, he was working nights [elsewhere] to help fund [the startup]. And they were pumping their own money in it and losing money. So [both founders] had full time jobs and started it up, and the jobs supported it and it was just kind of this visionary thing. And there's not a lot of young people who are crazy enough to do that. And the old ones like me, you know, I'm not going to work 24/7 for peanuts again. I spent my whole life working 24/7 for peanuts, it's lots of ways I can make money doing journalism or something similar to it, so I'm going to make some money.

This journalist actually does not accept what many journalists in the startup scene claim to embrace: working long hours for little or no pay. We find a common answer, in relation to the question what makes an entrepreneur an entrepreneur, is that it is "hard work" (and therefore comes with all kinds of sacrifices, particularly in the realm of economic and emotional security), like this quote we also use above to illustrate how journalists aim to create a workstyle:

That was another thing that I knew it was a startup, we were all doing very long hours, because we knew we had to maintain the site and we had to keep on top of the news as best as we can. That was another thing, editorial selection. We couldn't write everything, every story, just because of the … we didn't have enough people. That was another way I knew [it was a startup].

Brouwers and Witschge (2019) explore how in the discourses on both journalism and entrepreneurship there is an (implicit) norm that "it never stops." The culture of long working hours gets justified and naturalized by statements that either suggest this is "just the way it is," or that deliberately downplay the downsides of (over-)working in this industry, focusing on the joy and pleasure experienced. As this quote from one of the interviewees illustrates, for many journalists the number of hours on the job is not something they question. It is something that comes with a commitment to making a difference:

> I really don't know what free time is. I mean, I never really since I got into journalism, had free time. Even when I was on vacation, I was always writing, it never stopped. It's not something that you stop doing.

MAKING THE IMPOSSIBLE POSSIBLE?
Alaska Dispatch (United States)

Some of the startups started in basements where they had no phone reception; the *Alaska Dispatch News* started in a hangar. "That was where [the owner and publisher] kept her airplanes, so she had some extra space on the other side of the hangar," one of the journalists recounts. Another journalist remembers: "it was pretty bare bones." In addition, they were located at the far end of the world, in Anchorage, Alaska. Despite their challenges, the *Alaska Dispatch News* actually did very well for quite some time.

The founder had a vision, was a strong communicator and an excellent newsman. As people were getting laid off in local journalism, he saw an opportunity to fill gaps in politics and energy reporting, as well as create a space for investigative journalism that was of great importance to the local readership: "That was probably one of the biggest reasons why I started, it was just a place to put my own reporting on the corruption scandal at the time."

Specific Alaskan issues that are "far away" and "different from those in the rest of the country" – such as the oil-dependent economy, government revenue, being on the front lines of climate change and the specific lifestyle of the Alaska native people – were also potential stories.

And so what started as a blog by someone working nights at FedEx to finance it, after a few years managed to acquire the main newspaper in the state: the *Anchorage Daily News*.

> Unfortunately, it didn't last. The founder left shortly after the merger in 2014 and the company filed for bankruptcy in 2017. Still, they defied legacy media organizations for at least some time: "as far as revenue we were right near the top of local websites in the country. And I think that it was just a lot of tenacity on the sales side and on the journalism side to capture eyeballs. I think that's what made the old *Dispatch* unique as compared to other places."

Such a perception – that things are just meant to be a certain way – we find more generally. There are numerous instances in which interviewees liken entrepreneurship to fate, discarding their agency in their career trajectory. This occurs, for instance, when they express how they got into it coincidentally, rather than with a specific plan to become an entrepreneur, or as a founder states: "It is something that happens to you." This sentiment is paramount:

> By virtue of starting [the startup], I guess I became an entrepreneur, but it wasn't like something I, it just kind of ... maybe it chose me more than I chose it.

Many of the journalists do not even necessarily identify with being an entrepreneur. In terms of journalism as (their personal) passion project they "just do what they love." As this quote illustrates, being an entrepreneur is not necessarily an identity that they strongly identify with:

> You know, I don't [feel like an entrepreneur]. Or I didn't until you wrote to me actually [with the invitation to participate in research about entrepreneurship]. And I was thinking, I guess I could be seen that way. I guess I am a very, very small-scale entrepreneur. But when I think of entrepreneurs, they have a goal that really focuses on money and for me, I focus more on lifestyle, to be honest. And I've gotten to a point where again because of the turmoil last year and, I mean I'm 35, I'm still young but I'm not going to be young forever, I do think I actually need to focus on the money side a little bit more. But my solution to focus on the money is to go find higher-paying jobs still doing what I love.

What this quote shows is the denying or downplaying of economic interests. Though entrepreneurship generally, and the ambitions and goals of startups in particular, are often connected to economic interests in academic, industry, and policy discourses, we do not find such a focus in our conversations with startup journalists – with the sole exception of California-based InkaBinka, for whom selling the technology and financial profit was the rationale to start it. At InkaBinka it is journalism that becomes a commercial tool in order to develop and sell the underlying technology – an algorithm that gathers news stories and information online to summarize the news in a visually attractive bullet point format. All the other small businesses we visited expressed other types of goals related to quality journalism, public service and trust, and community impact.

In defining entrepreneurial journalism, in education and scholarship, the focus is often on the ability to monetize content in innovative ways: entrepreneurship is often seen as an answer to the economic crisis in journalism (see, for instance, Briggs 2012). Indeed, one of the main issues in the field is the challenge of finding sustainable business models (Picard 2014), given the decreasing revenues from advertising, subscriptions, and sales (Phillips and Witschge 2012). None of the startups in our sample have a sustainable source of revenue that allows them to break even or turn a profit – with the possible exception of Mediapart in France. Mediapart secured a stable base of subscribing members after scoring several high-profile scoops over their legacy competitors (Wagemans, Witschge, and Deuze 2016). Generally speaking, the business model is an issue of profound concern. Yet in all the conversations about their organizations, economic interests are an issue lingering in the background. The focus seems to be much more on ideological motives (related to serving the public or striving for quality ideals in journalism) rather than the market logic that underlies the startup (see also Witschge and Harbers 2018a).

What we find is that many of the entrepreneurs are – as with other aspects related to traditional journalism – critical of legacy sources of revenue. They protest the push to attract the largest possible audience for the purpose of maximizing advertisement revenues, something the reporters and editors we met see as a defining property of mainstream media. A market orientation would affect the quality of the content, these journalists argue:

> This industrial revolution ... promotes an economic model that destroys the value of the information model and drives on entertainment. It is, so to say, a form of free publicity aimed at the audience, for which one needs page views and clicks, ... the audience, meaning the anonymous masses, demand content that is faster, more superficial, reaching more people, creating more buzz, and therefore [this is] a model of entertainment for me.

We see a charged response to the question of what the entrepreneurs deem most relevant to their work. A number of the interviewees decidedly reject adopting business models that would be based on the hosting of advertising on their platform. Using passionate language, they explain that advertisements are an infringement of their editorial independence and would mean the pursuit of the "wrong" aims, such as circulation instead of quality. In doing so, they reiterate an age-old debate in journalism about whether a truly free press is possible if it relies on the market for its success. Traditionally, news organizations addressed this conundrum by strictly separating editorial from business operations. However, in recent decades, this "Church versus State" divide has gradually disappeared, as reporters and editors are increasingly expected to perform dual tasks, take responsibility for the market operations of their employer, and contribute to the bottom line. Concrete examples of this are the rise of branded and sponsored content, native advertising, and other forms of newswork where the marketing and editorial professions converge.

Similarly, in the startups we visited, we often found little or no strict separation between the business and journalistic sides of the company, even though most of these fledgling companies endeavor to find new sources of revenue, such as grants, third-party funding, micropayments, membership programs, or even investing their own savings. All of this is done in the service of maintaining what they see as their core journalistic integrity and responsibility to society.

JOURNALISM IN SPITE OF A BUSINESS MODEL
MMU Radio (Uganda)

At MMU Radio money does not seem the primary concern. The editors, presenters and technicians at the community radio station are all volunteers. One of the news editors is willing to volunteer "for as long as they can keep me," because journalism is "doing something you have passion for."

One presenter even left his paid job at another radio station to join this university radio, expecting real change to come from this: "When they advertised MMU Radio, what impressed me most was the nature of the radio."

MMU Radio wants to serve the community through their journalism. The aim is to be "a kind of radio that reaches out to the community, and makes sure the community improves to a standard that everybody would appreciate."

During its first summer, two Belgian journalists came to Uganda to organize training at MMU Radio. They talked about different kinds of stories, the buildup of a radio show, and how to handle a microphone. Their approach to journalism was also different, says one of the news editors. In Uganda, they "really don't go to journalism schools" and "sometimes they're subjective. That they want to take one side."

The trainers were part of an organization in Belgium that provided initial funding to set up the radio station. For now, the project runs entirely on donated funds, mainly from outside the immediate community. The concept for MMU Radio included ideas to make community engagement also part of the business model. But they realize it costs a lot of money to set that up, so it is coming together slowly: "Initially, we had proposed a kind of a hub close to the radio, that would be kind of a resource center. The community members can come and use the resources at a fee. We thought of having a café, for the communities to come and use that café. But it's a gradual process."

Much like *social entrepreneurship* (see, for instance, Dacin, Dacin, and Tracey 2011) and the pursuit of innovation to further societal goals rather than economic or technological ones (see Krumsvik et al. 2019), the journalists we met focus on the significance of the social cause they are serving. Though highly aware of the economic context in which they operate and the precarity of it, many of the entrepreneurs emphasize how economic viability is not a goal in itself: it is a means to obtaining their journalistic goals. Or, as this quote (which is applicable to many of the organizations we researched) shows, the *lack* of economic viability means that they cannot obtain their journalistic ambitions in the way they envisage:

> We can execute one tenth of all the ideas we have.... We are only a small club, we don't have expertise on every issue, I am super-busy and [Colleague] has to do ten things at the same time. A lot of it remains discussing it and then hoping something will come of it, for we cannot do more yet. But the larger we become, the more we will eventually be able to do.

Filling the gap

The fact that these startup journalists are not focusing on economic gains in their startup does not mean that they do not operate like "entrepreneurs" in a broader sense. Indeed, they can be seen as true pioneers given their sense of experimentation, and the way they position themselves online at the forefront of media-related transformation. As with pioneer communities in general (see Hepp 2016), the startup journalists in our project expressed a clear sense of what they wish to contribute, how they wish to fill a certain gap that they identify in the journalistic market. They overwhelmingly tend to describe themselves as providing a much-needed alternative to legacy media, and in their work feel they are fulfilling an important need for society (see also Singer 2015). They strive to make a difference and argue that they are best suited to do so – exactly because they are not "locked in" the constraints and structures of the traditional newsroom. At times they deliberately stretch the ideological conceptualization of journalism, which presumes that journalism is there to "inform" the public, as this quote illustrates:

To inform lacks several things that can make journalism relevant. It lacks the interaction with your audience, the assistance in situating issues – interpretation, involvement – why it is important.

The startup journalists use terms such as being "stubborn" and "headstrong," referring to the reward of energy, inspiration, and impact that can come from deliberately operating outside the legacy media institutional framework. This belief in being able to do things differently also translates into the way in which content is built and business models are set up. Many of the startup journalists show a certain type of stubbornness that seems to be needed to believe in the company's ideas even when no one else does, and a faith that the assessment of the market and potential audiences is sound and worth the risks involved:

Mediapart's initial bet was that people are capable, want to pay, to have quality news, exclusive news, well done, with other resources, other people that people almost never hear elsewhere, but who are experts. And the other bet was that they would be willing to pay for long-form stories. And that went completely against the press at that time, because at that time the press online could only be for free and it could only be short news stories. So, what we created, it was simply because that offer didn't exist at the time and we were ready to try to turn the car in the opposite direction, to do long-form stories that people had to pay for.

What we see is that the discourse of "crisis" in journalism, primarily associated with a loss of capacity for news media to effectively form a fourth estate (originally next to the clergy, the nobility, and citizens, more recently conceived as sources of institutional power separated into legislative, executive, and judiciary branches), is posed as an opportunity for startups to thrive. As our respondents claim: "There are less journalists to control the powers that be" and this is put forward as a main argument for startups to be successful. Indeed, chaos and crisis are mentioned as important motivators for change in the media landscape:

You know, change is opportunity. It's also chaos and loss, but it is opportunity... . I think we're in chaos, but I always see that as opportunity. I tend to be optimistic, I think change is a good thing, but people are really uncomfortable with change.

The startup journalists show awareness of the relevance of their expertise, now that legacy media have laid off so many specialists:

> I think that because of some of the layoffs especially in energy and political reporting, myself and others that we knew that were helping out had expertise in those matters and we could fill a gap.

It is not only in specific areas of specialized journalism that startups aim to make a contribution. We also note how they aim to give voice to lesser-represented groups and sometimes set very specific targets for this:

> I'd like to by the end of the year have maybe eight or nine portraits of communities ... that are usually completely neglected by intelligentsia. Hahaha, so that's my goal.

This is particularly relevant in local journalism, which has suffered the most from the "crisis" in journalism in terms of job losses, budget cuts, or the canceling of local titles and broadcasts. Those involved in this type of local, hyperlocal, or community journalism are particularly aware of the void left by the retreat of reporters on the local level, as this quote illustrates:

> We were filling up a gap. Because not too many people cared about all the details of this area, other news outlets, they would only pick up some of the biggest things. Many little things would just go unnoticed. Like the street-level type of stories.

NOT QUITE THE SAME, NOT QUITE DIFFERENT
Common Reader (United States)

The *Common Reader* at Washington University is not really a university publication and it is not really a journalistic publication. It's just different. The initiator wanted the *Common Reader* to be "a little bit quirky and maybe a little bit off the beaten path," but "without it being pretentious, or you know, without it being affected or trying too hard to be hip."

Expertise and personal preferences guided the choice of topic for the first edition: "I write a lot about music, so music is a subject that interests me a lot, so I knew when I was going to start this magazine that there was going to be an issue on music. Plus, the fact is that the provost, who is sort of my boss for this journal, is a musician. He loves music. So, I knew one of the ways to make him happy early on about this project was to do an issue about music."

Similarly, one of the writers goes into neighborhoods not because they're necessarily newsworthy, but because she feels they are underreported. She wants to make them visible, to give voice to the people living there. As an academic, she also feels her contribution is different from journalism: "I feel like what I'm doing is more argumentation. It's less exposition, it's less about reporting what's going on."

Although she also tries to incorporate some of the more journalistic aspects into her writing. And most of the writers do or did have journalistic ambitions: wanting to become journalists or publish in media outlets such as the *Atlantic* or the *New Yorker*.

Overall, this makes the *Common Reader* similar to journalism, while it's not really journalism as you'd expect it elsewhere. A writer explains, the articles "are very interesting, but they're not the kinds of articles that would immediately capture your attention when you would just read the byline. They're ones where you'd have to sit down and consciously spend a couple of minutes reading it and then realize that it offered something you didn't know you wanted."

Another journalist working at the same local news startup (US-based Corner Media Group) explains how their startup is providing a "voice to these neighborhoods" that are normally only portrayed negatively from afar. And a third journalist at this startup explains how they are "challenging incumbent media" that are "not doing their duty as they are not covering what needs to be covered." We find a similar sentiment among those working for the community radio station MMU in Western Uganda, as one of the journalists involved explains:

> to someone from the community radio, and that is MMU, we would visit the villages, people practicing farming, growing matoke, cabbages, onions … there are so many farmers there. And they are not catered for by these radio stations, most of them we have around.

Setting the standard

It is in this particular setting, where traditional media are deemed to "fail," that the startup journalists we spoke to try to make a difference, and try to bring in innovation to whatever they see as lacking in the legacy media context. Many speak about wanting to change journalism as a profession and an industry, inspiring change in the field as a whole. It becomes clear that they do not simply want to critique the status quo – they validate their choices and motivations with loftier goals, aimed at journalism writ large:

> Next to being a journalistic medium, we are a creative laboratory. It is a creative laboratory with the idea that journalism can be a creative occupation, especially in this time in history that we believe offers so many incredible opportunities to create online, to reconsider forms of journalism, indeed to reconsider the whole history of journalism.

The above quote is also illustrative of the sense of community that the startup journalists portray: most of them are working in small groups or teams, or even on their own (yet still connected in networks of peers); it matters to them, however, that the insights they gain, the work that they do, and the way they make sense of it are shared more widely in the profession of journalism. They stress the importance of "doing things together," they explain how they aim to inspire each other, and are convinced that they can have more impact by joining forces. Indeed, one of the recurring themes is a sense of "aliveness" that they feel in being in this together with others. Especially in the writings of psychoanalysts Donald Winnicott and Jacques Lacan (see Ruti 2010), this sense of being alive and feeling real are considered to be that what allows people to be creative. Their suggestion – following the analysis of Mari Ruti (2010: 353) – "that existential instability and precariousness are the flipside of creativity" seems to be embodied by the working lives and meaning-making tactics of the participants in our case studies.

While creativity and experimentation may go hand in hand with the precarious environment from which these journalism startups operate, this does not mean that "anything goes," nor that the journalists involved let go of any and all accepted rules or standards for quality newswork. They speak explicitly about wanting to set certain standards in their particular area. The data journalism outfit Code for South Africa is a good example of this:

> But in terms in quantitative goals, like so many projects and so many organizations, I would like Code4SA to have facilitated a data movement... . Our objective is to make journalism more effective. And once they become more effective, we can step out of that space.

The data journalism scene is an interesting case in point, to explore more broadly how startups at the boundary of journalism are changing the field from the outside. As is also shown by Seth Lewis and Nikki Usher (2014) and Stefan Baack (2018), the ways in which data journalists collaborate and develop a mutual understanding with other data workers, such as civic hackers, has implications for journalism more broadly. In particular, the group of journalists who are experimenting with the ways in which they do journalism change the rules of the game. They not only envisage journalism differently but subsequently alter their practices – which in the case of these data journalists and civic technologists means developing an even stronger aspiration to work in the public interest. Given the prominent role datafication plays in journalism more widely, with data journalism as an important new genre in journalistic production (Anderson 2018), the impact of startups and reporters active in this scene on the profession as a whole would be interesting to follow closely.

Andreas Hepp and Wiebke Loosen (2018) provide insight into the ways in which we can understand the work of pioneers in journalism who are setting new standards. They provide six characteristics that define such professional pioneers. Professional pioneers "construct themselves as people who take a *'forerunner role'* within a certain profession and are accepted in this role by other members of their field"; "act as *intermediaries* ... who in their pioneering practices inter-relate between different spheres – often explicitly advocating for moving beyond their own field"; are "embedded within *communities of practice*"; "take on the role of an *organizational elite*"; employ *"experimenting practices"*; and "possess *imaginations of possible future scenarios"* (ibid.: 6, emphasis in original).

With our interviewees, we find that most of the startups fit into this category of pioneering journalists. The pioneering attitude does not mean the occupational ideology of journalism is altogether abandoned. As the data journalism example shows, core values such as operating in the public interest at times get further solidified rather than discarded. As pioneers, startups innovate and transform as much as they are "reinforcing existing journalistic modes and normative commitments" (Carlson and Usher 2016: 568). As in the research of Matt Carlson and Nikki Usher (2016: 566), among ten for-profit news startups, we find a "tension between change and stasis among actors competing to define the journalistic field." Being a pioneer in journalism involves a balancing act between traditional and so-called innovative conceptualizations and practices, and we find that traditional definitions of journalism are still very much informing the practices and self-understandings of the startup journalists. It is exactly this tension between transformation and reinforcement of values, standards, and practices that provides the productive pressure allowing the startups to function effectively within the field of journalism and to self-identify as critical outsiders.

PIONEERING DATA JOURNALISM
C4SA (South Africa)

Those working at C4SA really feel like they are pioneers in the journalism field: "In the fifteen months we've been around we have made tremendous strides. We are in the open data space, we are known as the pioneers. In data journalism. We are well known also as data journalism pioneers."

Experimentation has shaped their work since the beginning: "Over the period we realized that no one really cares about data. People care about being able to answer questions about issues that are important to them.... What is helping them make their own decisions, that is a lot more powerful."

So they are also pioneering the ways in which they present their journalism, creating tools that people can use to improve their daily lives, such as the Medicine Price Comparison Tool and the Domestic Workers Tool. The project on the salaries of domestic workers shows that they are indeed successful at this: "It was incredibly well received. We had tens of thousands of users. The story was published in twenty newspapers, five radio interviews, hundreds of comments. It was big."

For journalists such concrete impact forms a reason to join the startup, as one of the journalists explains: "wanting to make a difference, being a pioneer, doing something different, something new, working with cool people."

C4SA also inspires people to reinvent themselves, as this graphic designer explains: "I'm new to the whole data thing," but as she had "a long-standing interest in data visualization from a design and arts point of view," and seeing the available data journalism tools, she realized she could do much more, also with open data. "The work that C4SA is doing fits really in what I would like to achieve personally, which is making design that makes a difference."

Pioneering journalism

So what then do these journalists contribute, in this balancing act between change and continuation in the field? One, they show us the many faces of journalism: there is not just one journalism, there are many forms, and it is forever changing, forever becoming: each new form and practice of journalism adds to what we consider to be journalism. Our cases show that while their contexts are vastly different, the precariousness of the position that journalism startups find (and put) themselves in is as much a consequence as it is a result of their actions and self-understandings. This tension reinforces as much as it challenges existing ways of doing journalism, and helps us to consider the profession as both a coherent field and a dynamic system. It is this movement that propelled our interest in this project, and looking back it is also what produces the most energy around the concepts, themes, and practices our team has documented across the various countries and cases.

Second, the stories of these journalists tell us there are many different reasons for doing journalism. What is beyond doubt is that the startups want to make a difference, want to have an impact, which they do at different levels and in a wide variety of ways, ranging from informing individual farmers, to building communities, to making society at large aware of issues that are in the public interest. Wagemans, Witschge, and Harbers (2019) show how, when we consider the role and impact that journalists envisage for themselves and for their profession at large, we need to consider the specific economic, cultural, geographic, and political context in which these journalists operate (see also Nerone 2013). Such awareness of context allows us to gain more relevant insights concerning journalism as conceived in "alternative" ways: "what is activism in one context, is not necessarily so in another, what is an act of protest or labeled as subjective reporting in one instance, may be conceptualised as empowering audiences and watchdog reporting in another" (Wagemans, Witschge, and Harbers 2019: 560). What is "upholding traditional journalistic values" in one context is "innovation and pioneering" in another.

Third, our data show that traditional and pioneering practices and values are not necessarily mutually exclusive. Rather, the startup journalists combine and navigate between traditional and alternative values. As such, they challenge our understanding of the field: where we tend to categorize practices, values, and definitions as juxtaposed, our data suggest that for the practicing journalists there are no issues in mixing, matching, and remixing them. It made us once more aware that, as journalism scholars and educators, we would benefit greatly from a richer, more nuanced, and complex understanding of the field, one that would allow us to address tensions and express our doubts, and would provide more room for alternative vocabularies to address dynamism in the field (see also Costera-Meijer 2016; Witschge et al. 2019).

Last, we need a better understanding of what "digital" refers to in journalism and journalism studies. The term "digital" has become shorthand to address the many changes in the journalistic field, and its widespread use is indicative of the nearly exclusive focus on technology when researching innovation in journalism. We find that change and transformation in journalism – whether relating to core values, associated practices, or ways of making sense of itself – in the digital realm relate to so much more than technology. In fact, one could argue innovation and change in journalism have as much if not more to do with emotion and affect regarding the work and the societal role of the profession than the distinct operations of computer interfaces and machines. Yes, technology is important – perhaps even essential – in the startups we researched. A broader understanding of the affordances of technology, however, should allow for and facilitate an appreciation of change beyond technological features. Peter Nagy and Gina Neff (2015: 1) remind us of how the role and impact of technologies tend to be determined by what people imagine these technologies to do (for them): "imagined affordances emerge between users' perceptions, attitudes, and expectations; between the materiality and functionality of technologies; and between the intentions and perceptions of designers." Even though we did not start out our investigations with this operational definition of affordance in mind, we can confirm how it opens up an embarrassment of riches when we look at all the different ways the startups in our sample use the digital context of their work to "make it work" in ways that are meaningful to them.

Taking on the role of rascals or rebels, these self-proclaimed crazy, sassy, and headstrong reporters, editors, and founders place themselves deliberately outside the mainstream, taking leeway to play with what is possible in journalism. They experiment and stretch the limits of journalism and do so in a highly productive way: they break free from the limited understanding of "who is a journalist" that has developed over time, while at the same time earning respect and claiming a place of recognition firmly located within journalism's occupational ideology and established ways of doing things. We do not suggest any of this is easy – it most certainly is not. While it is clear from our data that running a new journalistic venture is a daily struggle to survive economically, it is exactly this struggle that is part of the framework necessary for the kind of creativity and innovation that startup founders and participants find so meaningful. We are not blind to the precarity inherent to the startup context, yet we also cannot ignore the freedom and diversity that come with how these startups envisage and practice journalism. As one of the editors of a startup explains:

> There are a hundred different definitions of [strong journalism] as far as I'm concerned. It's being useful to the users, to the readers, it's explaining the world, it's accountability journalism that holds public institutions accountable, holding a mirror up to the community, it's providing strong breaking news coverage of events that are happening as they are happening.

Even though the definition of journalism this editor invokes is not necessarily brand new nor particularly innovative, what we find is that all these and other definitions of journalism upheld by the journalists we researched can exist side by side without obstructing the important work journalists do. The impact of startup journalism is that it opens journalism up to multiple imaginings, both in terms of what it does, and how it makes sense of itself.

Notes

Prologue: The Beyond Journalism Project

1 Source: https://www.svdj.nl/dutch-journalism-fund.
2 For other publications related to the Beyond Journalism project we refer to our names in the reference section of this book.
3 NWO-funded project "Understanding public participation: Journalism and democracy in a digital age" (236-45-005), participants of the Journalism Elsewhere project include: Laura Ahva, Chris Anderson, Stefan Baack, Florence Le Cam, Irene Costera Meijer, Mark Deuze, David Domingo, Wiebke Loosen, Julius Reimer, Karin Wahl-Jorgensen, Victor Wiard, Andy Williams, run by Tamara Witschge.
4 "Entrepreneurship at Work: Analysing practice, labour, and creativity in journalism" (funded by NWO, project number: 276-45-003, 2015–20); "Exploring Journalism's Limits: Enacting and theorising the boundaries of the journalistic field" (funded by NWO, project number: 314-99-205, 2017–19).

Introduction: What Is Journalism (Studies)?

1 This argument was made more broadly in an earlier article as: M. Deuze and T. Witschge (2018), Beyond journalism: Theorising the transformation of journalism. *Journalism* (18)3.

Chapter 1   The Becoming of Journalism

1   Source: http://pressthink.org.

Chapter 2   Setting the Scene: Startups

1   See, for example, the annual Global Entrepreneurship Monitor reports from 2006 onward: http://www.gemconsortium.org/report.
2   Examples can be found in the online database of journalism startups AngelList (angel.co/journalism) and MultipleJournalism (multiplejournalism.org).
3   https://www.gov.uk/government/publications/creative-industries-mapping-documents-1998.
4   https://www.rjionline.org/research/mark-deuze-and-tamara-witschge-fellowship-project-20152016.
5   With thanks to the researchers and graduate students involved: Hadewieg Beekman, Susan Blanken, Amanda Brouwers, Tessa Colen, Heleen d'Haens, Liz Dautzenberg, Alexandra van Ditmars, Luuk Ex, Sophie Frankenmolen, Renate Guitink, Ronja Hijmans, Victor Kuijpers, Boris Lemereis, Jorik Nijhuis, Guus Ritzen, Lotte van Rosmalen, Evelien Veldboom, Erik Verwiel, Charlotte Waaijers, Andrea Wagemans, Fleur Willems, Sofie Willemsen, Anki Witte, Milou van Zwan, Joris Zwetsloot.
6   http://newbeatsblog.com.
7   https://www.villamedia.nl/artikel/18.000-journalisten-in-nederland.
8   Special thanks to the research assistant and interviewer for the New Beats project: Nele Goutier.

References

Anderson, C. W. (2011) Blowing up the newsroom: Ethnography in an age of distributed journalism. In: D. Domingo and C. Paterson (eds.), *Making Online News, Vol. 2*, pp. 151–60. New York: Peter Lang.
———. (2014) The sociology of the professions and the problem of journalism education. *Radical Teacher* 99(2), pp. 62–8.
———. (2018) *Apostles of Certainty: Data Journalism and the Politics of Doubt*. Oxford: Oxford University Press.
Anderson, C. W., Bell, E., and Shirky, C. (2012) *Post-industrial Journalism: Adapting to the Present*. New York: Tow Center for Digital Journalism.
Audretsch, D. B. (2007) *The Entrepreneurial Society*. Oxford: Oxford University Press.
Baack, S. (2018) *Knowing what Counts: How Journalists and Civic Technologists Use and Imagine Data*. Groningen: RUG.
Bain, A. (2005) Constructing an artistic identity. *Work, Employment and Society* 19(1), pp. 25–46.
Banks, M. (2007) *The Politics of Cultural Work*. Basingstoke: Palgrave Macmillan.
Banks, M., Conor, B., and Mayer, V. (eds.) (2016) *Production Studies, The Sequel! Cultural Studies of the Global Media Industries*. New York: Routledge.
Banks, M., Taylor, S., and Gill, R. (eds.) (2013) *Theorizing Cultural Work*. London: Routledge.
Bantz, C., McCorkle, S., and Baade, R. C. (1980) The News Factory. *Communication Research* 7(1), pp. 45–68.
Bardoel, J. (1996) Beyond journalism: A profession between information society and civil society. *European Journal of Communication* 11(3), pp. 283–302.

Bauman, Z. (2000) *Liquid Modernity*. Cambridge: Polity.

———. (2005) *Liquid Life*. Cambridge: Polity.

Baym, N. K. (2015) Connect with your audience! The relational labour of connection. *The Communication Review* 18(1), pp. 14–22.

Bechky, B. (2011) Making organizational theory work: institutions, occupations, and negotiated orders. *Organization Science* 22(5), pp. 1157–67.

Beckett, C. (2010) *The Value of Networked Journalism*. London: Polis LSE.

Beckett, C. and Deuze, M. (2016) On the role of emotion in the future of journalism. *Social Media + Society* 2(3). Available at: http://journals.sagepub.com/doi/full/10.1177/2056305116662395.

Boltanski, L. and Thévenot, L. (2006) *On Justification: Economies of Worth*. Princeton: Princeton University Press.

Borger, M., Meijer, I. C., Van Hoof, A., and Sanders, J. (2013) "It really is a craft": Repertoires in journalistic frontrunners' talk on audience participation. *Medij. istraž* 19(2), pp. 31–54.

Bourdieu, P. (1998) *Acts of Resistance*. Cambridge: Polity.

Briggs, M. (2012) *Entrepreneurial Journalism*. New York: CQ Press.

Brouwers, A. (2017) Failure and understanding-with in entrepreneurial journalism. *Journal of Media Business Studies* 14(3), pp. 217–33.

Brouwers, A. and Witschge, T. (2019) "It never stops": The implicit norm of working long hours in entrepreneurial journalism. In: M. Deuze, M. Prenger (eds.), *Making Media*, pp. 441–51. Amsterdam: Amsterdam University Press.

Bruno, N. and Kleis Nielsen, R. (2012) *Survival Is Success: Journalistic Online Startups in Western Europe*. London: Tauris.

Burns, L. S. and Matthews, B. J. (2017) "Post-industrial" journalism as a creative industry. *International Journal of Social, Behavioral, Educational, Economic, Business and Industrial Engineering* 11(6), pp. 1543–51.

Cantillon, Z. and Baker, S. (2019) Affective qualities of creative labour. In: M. Deuze, M. Prenger (eds.), *Making Media*, pp. 287–96. Amsterdam: Amsterdam University Press.

Carlson, M. (2015) Introduction: The many boundaries of journalism. In: M. Carlson and S. Lewis (eds.), *Boundaries of Journalism: Professionalism, Practices and Participation*. London: Routledge.

Carlson, M. and Lewis, S. (2015) *Boundaries of Journalism: Professionalism, Practices and Participation*. Abingdon; New York: Routledge.

Carlson, M. and Usher, N. (2016) News startups as agents

of innovation: For-profit digital news startup manifestos as metajournalistic discourse. *Digital Journalism* 4(5), pp. 563–81.

Castells, M. (2010) *The Rise of the Network Society*. 3rd edition. Cambridge, MA and Oxford: Blackwell.

Chia, R. (1995) From modern to postmodern organizational analysis. *Organization Studies* 16(4), pp. 579–604.

Chia, R. and Holt, R. (2009) *Strategy without Design: The Silent Efficacy of Indirect Action*. Cambridge: Cambridge University Press.

Coates Nee, R. (2014) Social responsibility theory and the digital nonprofits: Should the government aid online news startups? *Journalism* 15(3), pp. 326–43.

Cohen, N. S. (2015) *Writers' Rights: Freelance Journalists in a Digital Age*. Montreal and Kingston: McGill-Queen's University Press.

———. (2018) At work in the digital newsroom. *Digital Journalism*, DOI: 10.1080/21670811.2017.1419821.

Compton, J. R. and Benedetti, P. (2010) Labour, new media and the institutional restructuring of journalism. *Journalism Studies* 11(4), pp. 487–99.

Conway, M. (2017) The ghost of television news in media history scholarship. *American Journalism* 34(2), pp. 229–39.

Corbett, A., Cornelissen, J., Delios, A., and Harley, B. (2014) Variety, novelty, and perceptions of scholarship in research on management and organizations: an appeal for ambidextrous scholarship. *Journal of Management Studies* 51(1), pp. 3–18.

Cornelissen, J. (2017) Preserving theoretical divergence in management research: why the explanatory potential of qualitative research should be harnessed rather than suppressed. *Journal of Management Studies* 54(3), pp. 368–83.

Costera-Meijer, I. (2001) The public quality of popular journalism: developing a normative framework. *Journalism Studies* 2(2), pp. 189–205.

Costera-Meijer, I. and Bijleveld, H. P. (2016) Valuable journalism. *Journalism Studies* 17(7), pp. 827–39.

Cottle, S. (2007) Ethnography and news production: new(s) developments in the field. *Sociology Compass* 1(1), pp. 1–16.

Couldry, N. (2004) Theorising media as practice. *Social Semiotics* 14(2), pp. 115–32.

Creech, B. and Nadler, A. M. (2018) Post-industrial fog: Reconsidering innovation in visions of journalism's future. *Journalism* 19(2), pp. 182–99.

Dacin, T., Dacin, P. A., and Tracey, P. (2011) Social entrepreneurship: a critique and future directions. *Organization Science* 22(5), pp. 1203–13.

Davidson, R. and Meyers, O. (2016) Should I stay or should I go? *Journalism Studies* 17(5), pp. 590–607.

De Maeyer, J. (2016) Adopting a "material sensibility" in journalism studies. In: T. Witschge et al. (eds.) *Sage Handbook of Digital Journalism*. London: Sage, pp. 460–76.

Delbridge, R. and Edwards, T. (2013) Inhabiting institutions: critical realist refinements to understanding institutional complexity and change. *Organization Studies* 34(7), pp. 927–47.

Deuze, M. (2003) The web and its journalisms: considering the consequences of different types of news media online. *New Media and Society* 5(2), pp. 203–30.

———. (2005) What is journalism? Professional identity and ideology of journalists reconsidered. *Journalism* 6(4), pp. 443–65.

———. (2007) *Media Work*. Cambridge: Polity.

———. (2019) The Netherlands: Making it work. In: M. Marjoribanks, L. Zion, P. O'Donnell, and M. Sherwood (eds.), *Journalists and Job Loss*. London: Routledge.

Deuze, M. and Witschge, T. (2017) What journalism becomes. In: C. Peters and M. Broersma (eds.), *Rethinking Journalism Again*, pp. 115–30. London: Routledge.

———. (2018) Beyond journalism: theorising the transformation of journalism. *Journalism Theory, Practice and Criticism* 19(2), pp. 165–81.

Deuze, M. and Prenger, M. (eds.) (2019) *Making Media*. Amsterdam: Amsterdam University Press.

Dimmick, J. and Coit, P. (1982) Levels of analysis in mass media decision-making: a taxonomy, research strategy, and illustrative data analysis. *Communication Research* 9(1), pp. 3–32.

Domingo, D. and Paterson, C. (2011) *Making Online News – Volume 2*. Bern, Switzerland: Peter Lang US.

Du Gay, P. (1996) *Consumption and Identity at Work*. London: Sage.

Duffy, B. E. (2016) The romance of work: Gender and aspirational labour in the digital culture industries. *International Journal of Cultural Studies* 19(4), pp. 441–57.

Ehrlich, M. C. (1995) The competitive ethos in television newswork. *Critical Studies in Mass Communication* 12(2), pp. 196–212.

Ekdale, B., Tully, S. H., and Singer, J. B. (2015) Newswork within a culture of job insecurity. *Journalism Practice* 9(3), pp. 383–98.

Ertel, M. et al. (2005) Adverse psychosocial working conditions and subjective health in freelance media workers. *Work and Stress* 19(3), pp. 293–9.

Fast, K. and Jansson, A. (2019) *Transmedia Work: Privilege and Precariousness in Digital Modernity*. London: Routledge.

Fast, K., Örnebring, H., and Karlsson, M. (2016). Metaphors of free labor: A typology of unpaid work in the media sector. *Media, Culture and Society* 38(7), pp. 963–78.

Feist, G. J. (1999) The influence of personality on artistic and scientific creativity. In: Sternberg, R. J. (ed.), *Handbook of Creativity*, pp. 273–96. Cambridge: Cambridge University Press.

Felski, R. (2015) *The Limits of Critique*. Chicago: The University of Chicago Press.

Fulton, J. (2015) Are you a journalist? New media entrepreneurs and journalists in the digital space. *Javnost – The Public* 22(4), pp. 362–74.

Gans, H. (2011) Multiperspectival news revisited: Journalism and representative democracy. *Journalism* 12(1), pp. 3–13.

Garnham, N. (2000) *Emancipation, the Media, and Modernity*. Oxford: Oxford University Press.

Gartner, W. B. (1989) "Who is an entrepreneur?" is the wrong question. *Entrepreneurship: Theory and Practice* 12(4), pp. 47–67.

———. (1993) Words lead to deeds: Towards emergency vocabulary. *Journal of Business Venturing* 8(3), pp. 231–9.

Görke, A. and Scholl, A. (2007) Niklas Luhmann's theory of social systems and journalism research. *Journalism Studies* 7(4), pp. 644–55.

Grabher, G. (2002) The project ecology of advertising: tasks, talents and teams. *Regional Studies* 36(3), pp. 245–62.

Grabher, G. and Thiel, J. (2015) Projects, people, professions: Trajectories of learning through a mega-event (the London 2012 case). *Geoforum* 65, pp. 328–37.

Haak, B. Van Der, Parks, M., and Castells, M. (2012) The future of journalism: Networked journalism. *International Journal of Communication* 6, pp. 2923–38.

Hallett, T. and Ventresca, M. (2006) Inhabited institutions. *Theory and Society* 35(2), pp. 213–36.

Hallin, D. C. (1992) The passing of the "high modernism" of American journalism. *Journal of Communication* 42(3), pp. 14–25.

Handy, C. (1998 [1989]) *The Age of Unreason*. Boston: Harvard Business School Press.

Hanitzsch, T. (2007) Deconstructing journalism culture: toward a universal theory. *Communication Theory* 17, pp. 367–85.

Hanitzsch, T. et al. (2011) Mapping journalism cultures across nations. *Journalism Studies* 12(3), pp. 273–93.

Hanitzsch, T., Vos, T. (2017) Journalism beyond democracy: a new look into journalistic roles in political and everyday life. *Journalism* 9(2), pp. 146–64.

Hanitzsch, T., Hanusch, F., Ramaprasad, J., and De Beer, A. S. (eds.) (2019) *Worlds of Journalism: Journalistic Cultures Around the Globe*. New York: Cambridge University Press.

Hartley, J. (1996) *Popular Reality: Journalism, Modernity and Popular Culture*. London: Arnold.

———. (2000) Communicational democracy in a redactional society: The future of journalism studies. *Journalism* 1(1), pp. 39–47.

Hartmann, M. (2009) The changing urban landscapes of media consumption and production. *European Journal of Communication* 24(4), pp. 421–36.

Heidegger, M. (2008[1927]) *Being and Time*. New York: HarperPerennial.

Heinonen, A., Koljonen, K. and Harju, A. (2017) From lay-offs to new beginnings: Experiences and emotions of journalists who were made redundant. Presentation at the NordMedia 2017 conference.

Heinrich, A. (2011) *Network Journalism: Journalistic Practice in Interactive Spheres*. London: Routledge.

Hellmueller, L. and Mellado, C. (2015) Professional roles and news construction: A media sociology conceptualization of journalists' role conception and performance. *Communication and Society* 28(3), pp. 1–11.

Hepp, A. (2016) Pioneer communities: collective actors in deep mediatisation. *Media, Culture and Society* 38(6), pp. 918–33.

Hepp, A. and Loosen, W. (2018) "Makers" of a future journalism? The role of "pioneer journalists" and "pioneer communities" in transforming journalism. *Communicative Figurations Working Paper* 19. Available at: http://www.zemki.uni-bremen.de/fileadmin/redak_zemki/dateien/Kofi-Arbeitspapiere/CoFi_EWP_No-19_Hepp-Loosen.pdf.

Hesmondhalgh, D. and Baker, S. (2011) *Creative Labour: Media Work in Three Cultural Industries*. London: Routledge.

Jenkins, H. (2006) *Convergence Culture: Where Old and New Media Collide*. New York: New York University Press.

Josephi, B. (2013) De-coupling journalism and democracy: Or how much democracy does journalism need? *Journalism* 14(4), pp. 441–5.

Karlsson, M., Clerwall, C. (2018) Transparency to the rescue? Evaluating citizens' views on transparency tools in journalism. *Journalism Studies* 19(13), pp. 1923–33.

Kosmala, K. (2007) The identity paradox? Reflections on fluid identity of female artists. *Culture and Organization* 13(1), pp. 37–53.

Kotišová, J. (2019) *Crisis Reporters, Emotions and Technology: An Ethnography*. London: Palgrave.

Kovach, B. and Rosenstiel, T. (2014) *The Elements of Journalism*. 3rd edition. New York: Crown.

Krumsvik, A. H., Milan, S., Niġ Bhroin, N. and Storsul, T. (2019)

Making (sense of) media innovations. In: Deuze, M., Prenger, M. (eds.), *Making Media*, pp. 193–206. Amsterdam: Amsterdam University Press.

Küng, L. (2015) *Innovators in Digital News*. London: I. B. Tauris and Co/Reuters Institute for the Study of Journalism.

Lakoff, G. and Johnson, M. (1980) *Metaphors We Live By*. Chicago: University of Chicago Press.

Landström, H. and Johannisson, B. (2001) Theoretical foundations of Swedish entrepreneurship and small-business research. *Scandinavian Journal of Management* 17, pp. 225–48.

Lefebvre, H. (1987) The everyday and everydayness. *Yale French Studies* 73, pp. 7–11.

Lewis, S. C. (2012) The tension between professional control and open participation: Journalism and its boundaries. *Information, Communication and Society* 15(6), pp. 836–66.

Lewis, S. C., Holton, A. E, and Coddington, M. (2014) Reciprocal journalism: A concept of mutual exchange between journalists and audiences. *Journalism Practice* 8(2), pp. 229–41.

Lewis, S. C. and Zamith, R. (2017) On the worlds of journalism. In: P. J. Boczkowski and C. W. Anderson (eds.), *Remaking the News: Essays on the Future of Journalism Scholarship in the Digital Age*. Cambridge, MA: MIT Press.

Löffelholz, M. and Weaver, D. (eds.) (2008) *Global Journalism Research*. Malden: Blackwell.

Lowe, G. F. and Brown, C. (eds.) (2016) *Managing Media Firms and Industries*. Berlin: Springer Scientific.

Malmelin, N. and Virta, S. (2016) Managing creativity in change. *Journalism Practice* 10(8), pp. 1041–54.

Manning-White, D. (1950) The "Gate Keeper": a case study in the selection of news. *Journalism Quarterly* 27(4), pp. 383–90.

Maxwell, R. (ed.) (2015) *The Routledge Companion to Labor and Media*. London: Routledge.

Mayer, V., Banks, M., and Caldwell, J. (2009) *Production Studies: Cultural Studies of Media Industries*. London: Routledge.

Mellado, C., Hellmueller, L., Márquez-Ramírez, M., Humanes, M. L., Sparks, C., Stepinska, A., Pasti, S., Schielicke, A., Tandoc, E., and Wang, H. (2017) The hybridization of journalistic cultures: A comparative study of journalistic role performance. *Journal of Communication* 67(6), pp. 944–67.

Mensing, D. H. and Ryfe, D. M. (2013) Blueprint for change: From the teaching hospital to the entrepreneurial model of journalism education. *#ISOJ* 2(2), pp. 144–61.

Michel, L. (2000) *Qualifikationsanforderungen in der professionellen Multimedia-Produktion*. Cologne: AIM.

Montuori, A. (2003) The complexity of improvisation and the

improvisation of complexity: Social science, art and creativity. *Human Relations* 56(2), pp. 237–55.

Mosco, V. (2009) The future of journalism. *Journalism* 10(3), pp. 350–2.

Nagy, P. and Neff, G. (2015) Imagined affordance: Reconstructing a keyword for communication theory. *Social Media + Society* 1(2).

Naldi, L. and Picard, R. G. (2012) "Let's start an online news site": Opportunities, Resources, strategy, and formational myopia in startups. *Journal of Media Business Studies* 4, pp. 47–59.

Neff, G., Wissinger, E., and Zukin, S. (2005) Entrepreneurial labor among cultural producers: "Cool" jobs in "hot" industries. *Social Semiotics* 15(3), pp. 307–34.

Nel, F. (2010) *Laid Off: What Do UK Journalists Do Next?* Preston: Journalism Leaders Programme, University of Central Lancashire.

Nerone, J. (2013) The historical roots of the normative model of journalism. *Journalism* 14(4), pp. 446–58.

Noordegraaf, M. (2007) From "pure" to "hybrid" professionalism: Present-day professionalism in ambiguous public domains. *Administration and Society* 39, pp. 761–85.

Oakley, K. (2014) Good work? Rethinking cultural entrepreneurship. In: Bilton, C. and Cummings, S. (eds.), *Handbook of Management and Creativity*. Cheltenham: Elgar, pp. 145–59.

O'Donnell, P., Zion, L., and Sherwood, M. (2015) Where do journalists go after newsroom job cuts? *Journalism Practice* 10(1), pp. 35–51.

Ornebring, H., Möller, C. (2018) In the margins of journalism: Gender and livelihood among local (ex-)journalists in Sweden. *Journalism Practice* 12(8), pp. 1051–60.

Ortega y Gasset, J. (1967) *The Origin of Philosophy*. Chicago: University of Illinois Press.

Pantti, M. (2010) The value of emotion: An examination of television journalists' notions on emotionality. *European Journal of Communication* 25(2), pp. 168–81.

Paterson, C. and Domingo, D. (2008) *Making Online News*. Bern, Switzerland: Peter Lang US.

Paterson, C. Lee, D., Saha, A. and Zoellner, A. (eds.) (2016) *Advancing Media Production Research: Shifting Sites, Methods, and Politics*. London: Palgrave.

Perren, A. and Holt, J. (eds.) (2009) *Media Industries: History, Method, and Theory*. Malden: Blackwell.

Peters, C. (2011) Emotion aside or emotional side? Crafting an "experience of involvement" in the news. *Journalism* 12(3), pp. 297–316.

Peterson, R. and Anand, N. (2004) The production of culture perspective. *Annual Review of Sociology* 30, pp. 311–34.

Phillips, A. and Witschge, T. (2012) The changing business of news. In: Lee-Wright, P., Phillips, A., and Witschge, T. (eds.), *Changing Journalism*. London: Routledge, pp. 3–20.

Picard, R. (2010) The biggest mistake of journalism professionalism. *The Media Business*, 1/2/10. Available at: http://themediabusiness. blogspot.com/2010/01/biggest-mistake-of-journalism.html.

———. (2014) Twilight or new dawn of journalism? *Journalism Studies* 15(5), pp. 500–10.

Podkalicka, A. and Rennie, E. (2018) *Using Media for Social Innovation*. Bristol: Intellect.

Polanyi, M. (1998) *The Logic of Liberty: Reflections and Rejoinders*. London: Routledge.

Powers, M. and Zambrano, S. V. (2016) Explaining the formation of online news startups in France and the United States: A field analysis. *Journal of Communication* 66, pp. 857–77.

Prenger, M. and Deuze, M. (2017) The structural history and theory of innovation and entrepreneurialism in journalism. In: Boczkowski, P., Anderson, C. (eds.), *Remaking the News*, pp. 235–50. Boston: MIT Press.

Reese, S. and Shoemaker, P. (2016) A media sociology for the networked public sphere: the hierarchy of influences model. *Mass Communication and Society* 19, pp. 389–410.

Reinardy, S. (2009) Female journalists more likely to leave newspapers. *Newspaper Research Journal* 30(3), pp. 42–57.

———. (2011) Newspaper journalism in crisis: Burnout on the rise, eroding young journalists' career commitment. *Journalism* 12(1), pp. 33–50.

Rodrigues, C. and Baroni, A. (2018) Journalism ethos: Mídia Ninja and a contested field. *Brazilian Journalism Research* 14(2), pp. 568–93.

Rossiter, N. (2006) *Organized Networks: Media Theory, Creative Labour, New Institutions*. Rotterdam: Nai Publishers.

Ruotsalainen, J. (2018) Scanning the shape of journalism – Emerging trends, changing culture? *Futures*. Available at: https:// doi.org/10.1016/j.futures.2018.06.011

Russell, A. (2015) Networked journalism. In: Witschge, T., Anderson, C. W., Domingo, D., et al. (eds.), *The Sage Handbook of Digital Journalism*. New York: Sage, pp. 149–63.

Ruti, M. (2010) Winnicott with Lacan: Living creatively in a postmodern world. *American Imago* 67(3), pp. 353–74.

Ryfe, D. (2012) *Can Journalism Survive?* Cambridge: Polity.

Sartre, J. P. (1976) *Critique of Dialectical Reason* (trans. A. Sheridan-Smith). London: NLB.

Schaffer, J. (2010) *New Voices: What Works*. J-Lab: The Institute for Interactive Journalism, Washington, D.C.

Scholl, A. and Weischenberg, S. (1998) *Journalismus in der Gesellschaft. Theorie, Methodologie und Empirie*. Opladen/ Wiesbaden: Westdeutscher Verlag.

———. (1999) Autonomy in journalism: How it is related to attitudes and behavior of media professionals. *Web Journal of Mass Communication Research* 2(4). Available at: http://www. scripps.ohiou.edu/wjmcr/vol02/2-4a-B.htm.

Schudson, M. (1995) *The Power of News*. Cambridge: Harvard University Press.

———. (2003) *The Sociology of News*. New York: W. W. Norton.

———. (2008) *Why Democracies Need an Unlovable Press*. Cambridge: Polity.

Sennett, R. (2006) *The Culture of the New Capitalism*. New Haven: Yale University Press.

———. (2008) *The Craftsman*. New Haven: Yale University Press.

Sherwood, M. and O'Donnell, P. (2018) Once a journalist, always a journalist? *Journalism Studies* 19(7), pp. 1021–38.

Siapera, E. (2019) Affective labour and media work. In: Deuze, M. and Prenger, M. (eds.), *Making Media*, pp. 287–96. Amsterdam: Amsterdam University Press.

Siapera, E. and Iliadi, I. (2015) Twitter, journalism and affective labour. *About Journalism* 4(1), pp. 76–89.

Simons, M. (ed.) (2013) *What's Next in Journalism?* Brunswick, VIC, Australia: Scribe.

Sørensen, B. M. (2008) "Behold, I am making all things new": The entrepreneur as savior in the age of creativity. *Scandinavian Journal of Management* 24, pp. 85–93.

Sparks, C. (1991) Goodbye, Hildy Johnson: the vanishing "serious press." In: Dahlgren, P. and Sparks, C. (eds.), *Communication and Citizenship*, pp. 57–72. London: Routledge.

Stearns, J. (2013) *Acts of Journalism: Defining Press Freedom in the Digital Age*. New York: Free Press.

Steensen, S., Ahva, L. (2015) Theories of journalism in a digital age. *Journalism Practice* 9(1), pp. 1–18.

Štěpánková, R. (2015) The experience with a person with autism: Phenomenological study of the experience with contact and contact reflections. *Person-Centered and Experiential Psychotherapies* 14(4), pp. 310–27.

Storey, J., Salaman, G., and Platman, K. (2005) Living with enterprise in an enterprise economy: Freelance and contract workers in the media. *Human Relations* 58(8), pp. 1033–54.

Storsul, T. and Krumsvik, A. (eds.) (2013) *Media Innovations: A Multidisciplinary Study of Change*. Gothenburg: Nordicom.

Timmermans, S. (2015) Introduction: Working with Leigh Star.

In: Bowker, G. C., Timmermans, S., Clarke, A. E., et al. (eds.), *Boundary Objects and Beyond*. Cambridge, MA: MIT Press, pp. 1–9.

Tuchman, G. (1978) *Making News*. New York: Free Press.

Tunstall, J. (1971) *Journalists at Work*. London: Constable.

Ullman, E. (1997) *Close to the Machine: Technophilia and Its Discontents*. San Francisco: City Lights.

Usher, N. (2014) *Making News at the New York Times*. Ann Arbor: University of Michigan Press.

———. (2017) Venture-backed news startups and the field of journalism. *Digital Journalism* 5(9), pp. 1116–33.

Vázquez Schaich, M. J. and Klein, J. S. (2013) Entrepreneurial journalism education: Where are we now? *Observatorio* 7(4), pp. 185–211.

Verschuren, P. (2003) Case study as a research strategy: Some ambiguities and opportunities. *International Journal of Social Research Methodology* 6(2), pp. 121–39.

Villi, M. and Picard, R. (2018) Transformation and innovation of media business models. In: Deuze, M. and Prenger, M. (eds.), *Making Media*, pp. 121–32. Amsterdam: Amsterdam University Press.

Vinken, H. (2017) *Monitor Freelancers en Media 2016*. Tilburg: Pyrrhula/NVJ.

———. (2018) *Monitor Freelancers en Media 2017*. Tilburg: Pyrrhula/NVJ.

von Rimscha, B. (2015) The impact of working conditions and personality traits on the job satisfaction of media professionals. *Media Industries Journal* 2(2). Available at: http://dx.doi.org/10.3998/mij.15031809.0002.202.

Vos, T. P. and Singer, J. B. (2016) Media discourse about entrepreneurial journalism. *Journalism Practice* 10(2), pp. 143–59.

Wagemans, A., Witschge, T., and Deuze, M. (2016) Ideology as resource in entrepreneurial journalism. *Journalism Practice* 10(2), pp. 160–77.

Wagemans, A., Witschge, T., and Harbers, F. (2019) Impact as driving force of journalistic and social change. *Journalism* 20(4), pp. 552–67.

Wahl-Jorgensen, K. (2009) News production, ethnography, and power: On the challenges of newsroom-centricity. In: Bird, E. (ed.), *The Anthropology of News and Journalism: Global Perspectives*. Bloomington: Indiana University Press, pp. 21–35.

Weaver, D. and Willnat, L. (eds.) (2012) *The Global Journalist in the 21st Century*. London: Routledge.

Westlund, O. and Lewis, S. C. (2014) Agents of media innovations: Actors, actants, and audiences. *The Journal of Media Innovations* 1(2), pp. 10–35.

Willnat, L., Weaver, D., and Choi, J. (2013) The global journalist in the twenty-first century. *Journalism Practice* 7(2), pp. 163–83.

Windahl, S. and Rosengren, K. E. (1978) Newsmen's professionalization: Some methodological problems. *Journalism Quarterly* 55(3), pp. 466–73.

Witschge, T. (2013) Transforming journalistic practice: A profession caught between change and tradition. In: Peters, C. and Broersma, M. (eds.), *Rethinking Journalism: Trust and Participation in a Transformed News Landscape*. London: Routledge, pp. 160–72.

Witschge, T., Anderson, C. W., Domingo, D. and Hermida, A. (2019) Dealing with the mess (we made): Unraveling hybridity, normativity, and complexity in journalism studies. *Journalism* 20(5), pp. 651–9.

Witschge, T. and Harbers, F. (2018a) The entrepreneurial journalist. In: Eldridge, S. and Franklin, B. (eds.), *The Routledge Handbook of Developments in Digital Journalism Studies*. London: Routledge, pp. 86–98.

———. (2018b) Journalism as practice. In: Vos, T. (ed.), *Journalism. Handbooks of Communication Studies Vol. 19*. Berlin: De Gruyter Mouton, pp. 105–23.

Witschge, T. and Nygren, G. (2009) Journalism: A profession under pressure? *Journal of Media Business Studies* 6(1), pp. 37–59.

Wrona, T. and Gunnesch, M. (2016) The one who sees more is more right: How theory enhances the "repertoire to interpret" in qualitative case study research. *Journal of Business Economics* 86, pp. 723–49.

Ybema, S. (2003) *De koers van de krant*. Amsterdam: Vrije Universiteit.

Zelizer, B. (2004) *Taking Journalism Seriously*. London: Sage.

———. (2013) On the shelf life of democracy in journalism scholarship. *Journalism* 14(4), pp. 459–73.

———. (2016) *What Journalism Could Be*. Cambridge: Polity.

Zelizer, B. and Allan, S. (eds.) (2011) *Journalism after September 11*. London: Routledge.

Zion, L. et al. (2016) Working for less: The aftermath for journalists made redundant in Australia between 2012 and 2014. *Communication Research and Practice* 2(2), pp. 117–36.

Index